Overcoming Problematic Alcohol and Drug Use

A Guide for Beginning the Change Process

Jeremy M. Linton

Routledge
Taylor & Francis Group
New York   London

Routledge
Taylor & Francis Group
270 Madison Avenue
New York, NY 10016

Routledge
Taylor & Francis Group
2 Park Square
Milton Park, Abingdon
Oxon OX14 4RN

© 2008 by Taylor & Francis Group, LLC
Routledge is an imprint of Taylor & Francis Group, an Informa business

Printed in the United States of America on acid-free paper
10 9 8 7 6 5 4 3 2 1

International Standard Book Number-13: 978-0-415-96072-4 (Softcover)

Visit the Taylor & Francis Web site at
http://www.taylorandfrancis.com

and the Routledge Web site at
http://www.routledge.com

For my children,

Caroline Rose, Jon Henry, and Madeline Lee

May you live safe, long, and healthy lives

CONTENTS

PREFACE

The question "Why another book about alcohol and drugs?" is not a difficult one to answer. To put it simply, the problem of alcohol and other drug (AOD) abuse in the United States is as vast and far-reaching as it has ever been. Researchers from the Substance Abuse and Mental Health Services Administration (SAMHSA), the National Institute on Drug Abuse (NIDA), the Center for Substance Abuse Treatment (CSAT), and other organizations continue to report astounding rates of AOD abuse patterns. It is also no longer a secret that AOD abuse affects people of all ages and from all walks of life. Gone are the stereotypes of skid-row alcoholics or inner-city crack addicts as the only AOD abusers. Without a doubt, alcohol and drug abuse problems know no boundaries.

Historically, treatment for AOD problems has been based on the disease model of addiction. According to the disease model, AOD abuse is a chronic, progressive, and genetic disease that, if left untreated, will result in death (Doweiko, 2006). The disease model was also the basis for the 12-steps of Alcoholics Anonymous (AA), Narcotics Anonymous (NA), and other such support groups. Although treatment based on the disease concept and the 12-steps have helped thousands recover from AOD problems, it has also failed to help others. Clearly, continued developments in the area of treatment are necessary to combat our nation's problem with AOD.

Although the disease model of AOD abuse and the 12-steps of recovery are mentioned only briefly in this book, I do not deny their important place in the world of AOD treatment. Rather, the purpose of this book is to provide a different approach for addressing AOD problems, one that is based on years of research and practice. When used in the right ways by treatment providers, the methods described in this book have been shown time and time again to be helpful to clients in AOD counseling. If you have previous experience with the disease model and 12-steps as a method of treatment, be it as a client or clinician, I urge you to keep an open mind as you work through this book.

This is an exciting time in the AOD abuse treatment field. Recognizing the shortcomings of the disease model of addiction and the related treatment approaches, several researchers and treatment professionals have created other forms of treatment for AOD problems. These include the use of Aaron Beck and colleagues' (2001) *Cognitive Therapy of Substance Abuse*, Prochaska and DiClemente's (1994) *The Transtheoretical Approach: Crossing Traditional Boundaries of Therapy*, Miller and Rollnick's (2001) *Motivational Interviewing*, the principles of relapse prevention and harm reduction treatment offered by G. Alan Marlatt and D. Donovan (2002, 2005), and solution-focused brief counseling (Berg & Miller, 1992). Each of these models of treatment emphasizes respect, a focus on strengths, the importance of personal choice, and self-determination of goals for the person struggling with AOD abuse. These models are also the foundation on which this book was written.

I first became aware of the need for alternative AOD treatment approaches early in my career as a counselor in a maximum security prison. Many of the clients that I worked with behind the prison walls were sentenced to spend the rest of their lives locked up with no hope of being free again. Although these men wanted to make positive changes in their lives, including goals to quit using alcohol and drugs (yes, AOD is available inside prisons), they found no comfort in AA/NA meetings and 12-step treatment approaches. The main aspect of the 12-step approaches that many of my prison clients had difficulty with was the need to rely on a Higher Power to attain sobriety. As one client asked, "How can I give myself over to a Higher Power that lets places like this prison live on?" Having no good answer for this client, I began my search for an approach that could more effectively help him meet his goals.

My search took me to the concepts outlined in this book. Since my first prison job, I have witnessed firsthand the effectiveness of these newer treatment approaches. I have employed these approaches with success in prisons and jails, residential treatment centers, agency settings, and private practice. I have also supervised and taught counselors-in-training to use these approaches and have seen my students' success with clients. It is for these reasons that I felt compelled to write this book.

Whoever you are and for whatever reason you have selected this book, you are to be commended for committing yourself to change. As you work on the concepts in the chapters that follow, I wish you luck in achieving your goals. Work hard and enjoy the positive changes that you create!

ABOUT THE AUTHOR

Jeremy M. Linton, Ph.D. is program chair and assistant professor of counseling and human services at Indiana University South Bend where he teaches and conducts research in the area of substance abuse counseling. In addition, Dr. Linton is a consulting mental health counselor at Samaritan Counseling Center in South Bend, Indiana, and Clinical Supervisor for Western Michigan University's Substance Abuse Clinic. Dr. Linton has provided substance abuse and mental health counseling services in prisons and jails, community agencies, and private practice. He is a licensed mental health counselor and has advanced training in substance abuse and couples and family counseling. Dr. Linton regularly conducts trainings on substance abuse counseling and supervises students working in substance abuse counseling settings.

1

DETERMINING YOUR GOALS AND GETTING STARTED

Welcome to this book! This opening chapter is designed to help you take some first steps toward change. There are several questions for thought and activities to complete as you work through this chapter. By the end of this chapter you should:

1. Have a good idea about the purpose of this book.
2. Have some goals for change.
3. Understand why you want to change.
4. Understand the pros and cons for change.
5. Be ready to put your full energy into completing the rest of this book.

Good luck!

PURPOSE OF THIS BOOK

If you have picked up this book, then you are interested in doing something about the problem of alcohol and drugs. You may be a person trying to cope with an alcohol and other drug abuse (AOD) problem and have selected this book to help you change your patterns of AOD use. Or, you may be a counselor looking for new ways to address substance abuse issues with your clients. Finally, you may be a counselor-in-training learning about alcohol and drug abuse for the first time. This book is appropriate for all such readers. A little bit later in this chapter, I will offer some suggestions for how each type of reader can effectively use the content of this book.

The first question to think about is, *Why read this book instead of some other book on alcohol and drug abuse?* Simply put, this book summarizes much of what we know about change, and it guides you through the process of putting theories of change into action. Presented in the chapters that follow are key concepts about change developed by leading researchers in the substance abuse treatment field. This means that you can benefit from years of research conducted all over the world.

This book is comprised of nine chapters covering different aspects of recovery from AOD abuse problems. The chapters should be used in order, and concepts in later chapters build off those presented in earlier chapters. As you work through this book you will notice several special features included in each chapter. Classic research on learning tells us that people learn new information best when they engage the material on four different levels (Kolb, 1981). These levels include: (a) hearing or reading new information, (b) understanding why the material is relevant to the learner's personal life, (c) practicing new skills related to the information, and (d) reflecting on each of the proceeding tasks. Each chapter of this book is designed to provide the reader with opportunities to experience the material on all of these levels.

Each chapter of this book begins by providing the reader with relevant information on the chapter topic. Following this, throughout each chapter, several features are included to promote the reader's active engagement with the material. These include *examples* to promote a concrete understanding of the topic, *questions for thought* to encourage reflection on what is learned, and *chapter assignments* to encourage practice of new skills. In order to get the full benefit from this book it will be very important for you to actively take part in each of these activities.

OPENING QUESTIONS

Now it's time to get to work! Let's start with an easy question: *Why have you picked up this book?* Probably, the answer to this question is that, for whatever reason, you desire to make some sort of change. If this is true for you, the questions become: *What is it about your life that you want to be different?* and *Why do you want to change?* Either you have decided on your own that you want to make changes to your alcohol and drug use patterns or someone else has decided for you that you need to do so. Maybe you have examined your life and decided that your current pattern of alcohol and drug use no longer works for you. Perhaps a loved one has told you to seek some kind of help for your alcohol or drug use in the form of an ultimatum; either get help or our relationship is over. Possibly, your employer has urged you to take a look at your alcohol and drug use. Or, maybe you are just curious about your drug and alcohol use and have decided to investigate whether you have a problem. Whatever your motivation, I offer my congratulations! You have picked up this book and have at least committed to exploring the possibility of change. Now, let's move on and think about the questions that I asked above.

WHAT TYPE OF USER ARE YOU?

An important task in thinking about changing your AOD use patterns is to figure out what type of AOD user you are. Different people use alcohol and drugs at different rates and experience different consequences of their use. The nature of your relationship with AOD and the types of consequences you have experienced because of your use will have a direct impact on the plans you make throughout the rest of this book.

To help you better understand the type of AOD user you are, we can turn to the scientific research in the field. Miller and Munoz (2005), two well-respected researchers in the area of AOD treatment, identified four different patterns of alcohol use: overdrinking, dumb drinking, harmful drinking, and dependent drinking. Because this book is about overcoming both alcohol and drug use, Miller and Munoz's categories have been slightly modified to include the use of other drugs in addition to alcohol. Each is described below.

Overusing

Overusing involves taking more alcohol or drugs than is considered physically safe. At certain levels, for example, alcohol has no harmful physical effects on the body. For men, this safe level of drinking is two drinks per day and for women it is one drink per day. However, when you drink more than this, you put yourself at a higher risk for harmful physical consequences such as liver and digestive problems, respiratory distress, and high blood pressure. With other drugs, however, there is no safe level of use. Smoking marijuana, for instance, even occasionally, is harmful to your lungs. Likewise, taking oxycodone without a prescription and supervision from a physician is equally as dangerous.

It is important to note that overusers may not experience any harmful effects of their AOD use. They may avoid legal difficulties, family conflict, problems at work, and any other related stressors. Similarly, they may not even experience any harmful physical effects of their AOD use. However, the danger lies in the fact that the overuser is placing him- or herself at a higher risk for harmful consequences and therefore needs to take a look at his or her patterns of use.

Dumb Using

In the next category, dumb using, the user takes AOD in situations where it is dangerous or unadvisable to do so. Miller and Munoz (2005) offer drinking alcohol before driving as the classic example of dumb using. Even at very low levels, alcohol can impair the user's ability to safely operate an automobile. Simply put, drinking before driving, even if only done one time, is dumb.

For the most part, use of drugs other than alcohol can almost always be categorized as dumb use. Even if users are merely experimenting for the first time with a drug, they are placing themselves at a high risk for negative consequences. People's bodies react differently to different drugs, and what may be safe for one user can be deadly for another. Taking a drug without knowing how it will affect you is like playing Russian roulette, and to do so is not smart. A famous example of this came in 1986 with the death of college basketball great Bias. Less than 48 hours after being selected in the 1986 NBA draft, Len Bias died of a cardiac arrhythmia induced by cocaine use. It is unclear if Bias was a regular cocaine user. However, because he had a preexisting heart condition, this a tragedy that could have occurred even if Bias had only used cocaine on this one occasion.

Experimental or occasional use of marijuana and other drugs thought by some (erroneously!) to be relatively harmless can also be categorized as dumb use. With the advent of more potent strains of marijuana, the trading business for this drug has become more and more intense. In an effort to keep up with more powerful strains of the drug, some manufacturers and dealers have elected to cut their marijuana with other drugs (e.g., PCP, LSD, or cocaine) or harmful chemicals. In effect, this has led to a "buyer beware" situation for marijuana users; you never really know what you are going to get when you purchase the drug. As a result, the marijuana user may be ingesting several toxins, in addition to those present in the marijuana, which could lead to many harmful consequences.

Harmful Using

The third category of use described by Miller and Munoz (2005) is harmful using. In this category, AOD users are experiencing actual harm or problems from their use, not just placing themselves at a higher risk as in the previous two categories. The hallmark of harmful using is that the users' problems are a direct result of their AOD use. Problems created by AOD use in this category may include conflict in relationships, missing work, legal troubles, or AOD-related health problems. For whatever reason, however, the user keeps taking AOD in the face of these consequences.

Dependent Using

Finally, there is dependent using. Miller and Munoz (2005) describe this category of use as being characterized by either physical dependence or psychological dependence on AOD. Physical dependence occurs when the user needs more and more of the drug to get high and experiences symptoms of withdrawal when the drug is not present in their system. Psychological dependence comes about when the user feels like he or she cannot function without the drug. In both cases, the dependent user has given up many enjoyable activities and spends more and more time drinking or using drugs. For dependent users, AOD has become the central part of their daily lives and they continue to use despite many harmful consequences.

Questions for Thought

1. Which category of use do you think you are in?
2. What characteristics of the category best match with your AOD use patterns?
3. What is your reaction to this assessment?

Keep your answers to these questions in mind as you work through the rest of this chapter.

WHAT DO YOU WANT TO CHANGE?

Now that you have thought about the type of AOD user you are, let's think about change. If you are ready or willing to consider change, what is it that you want to change? For some, the answer to this question is easy. For others, the answer is more difficult to come up with. In either case, take some time to think about this question. It has been said that if you don't know where you are going you will never know if you get there. This is especially true for those who want to change their alcohol and drug use patterns. You must understand what you want to see difference in your life before you can start trying to change. One important question to consider, for example, is whether you want to quit using AOD all-together or reduce the amount you use.

In answering the question of what you want to change you may find it helpful to write your ideas down. Use Worksheet 1 at the end of this chapter to begin thinking about this question. When completing this worksheet, take your time and think hard about what it is you want to change. Your answers on Worksheet 1 will be the foundation upon which the rest of this book is built.

As you complete Worksheet 1, be as specific and detailed as possible when writing down your answers. For example, maybe you want to reduce the amount of alcohol that you drink. This is a good goal to begin with, but I would encourage you to be more specific in your response. Do you want to drink alcohol on fewer days of the week? Do you want to consume fewer drinks per sitting? Or, do you want to not drink at all. An example may help here.

Example: Frank decided he wants to reduce the amount of beer he drinks. For now, he has decided that he does not want to quit drinking beer all together, just the number of beers he drinks per week. Frank set as his goal to reduce the number of drinks he consumes per sitting and the number of days that he drinks per week. Currently, Frank drinks 6 days per week. He decides that he wants to drink a maximum of 3 days per week and wants to consume a maximum of 3 beers per drinking day. With this goal in mind, Frank was fairly confident that he could be successful.

Hopefully this example helps. Take some time before proceeding with the chapter to jot down on Worksheet 1 specific things you want to change. Once you have finished, move on to the next section.

WHY CHANGE?

Having now set some goals for change, it is time to figure out why you want to change. In other words, what is your motivation for wanting to change? Some think that people will be successful at changing only if they want it themselves. When people are motivated to change for their own personal reasons we call this *intrinsic motivation*. However, the idea that only intrinsically motivated persons are successful at changing is false. Time and time again, research has shown that people who are not intrinsically motivated change at the same rates as those who are motivated by reasons other than their own (when this happens we call it *extrinsic motivation*). So, whatever your reasons are for trying to change, you have a good possibility of being successful. Use Worksheet 2 to write down your answers to the question: *Why do you want to change?*

WHAT ARE THE POSITIVES AND NEGATIVES OF CHANGE?

With most things there are positive and negative aspects to change, and alcohol and drug use is no different. Simply put, if you did not receive positive benefits from AOD you would be less likely to use them. Therefore, it is safe to assume that you have, in the past, received some positive benefits as a result of your problematic AOD use. As you think about change it is important to acknowledge that there are positives and negatives to changing your AOD use.

Miller and Rollnick (2001) created a decisional balance chart to help identify the positives and negatives of change. You can find this chart in Worksheet 3 at the end of this chapter. On the left-hand side of the chart, write down all the possible benefits of changing your AOD use patterns. On the right side, write down all the possible benefits of not changing your use patterns and maintaining the current status quo. An example may help here.

Example: Julie is thinking about quitting her use of marijuana. As she thinks about it, she realizes that there are some things that she likes about smoking marijuana and worries that it will be difficult to give up. She decides to complete the decisional balance chart to help her think about this problem a bit more. Her answers are below.

Benefits of Change	Benefits of Staying the Same
I'd have more money	It's what I have always done
I might be able to breathe better	I might have to find new friends
My parents might not be so disappointed in me	It's fun to smoke with friends and laugh a lot
I would not have to worry about dirty drug screens on job interviews	It helps me sleep at nightIt helps me deal with the stress of day-to day life
I'd have more energy to play volleyball	
I might sleep less	
I might lose some weight	
I'd feel better about myself and not like such a loser	

Questions for Thought

1. Was working on your decisional balance chart difficult for you?
2. If yes, why?
3. Which side of the chart has a longer list?
4. What are your thoughts after completing the chart?
5. Was this activity helpful to you? Why or why not?

HOW CONFIDENT ARE YOU THAT YOU CAN CHANGE?

A final question I would like you to consider in this chapter relates to your level of confidence in your ability to change. Insoo Kim Berg and Scott Miller (1992), two well-respected researchers and practitioners, say that they often ask their clients the following:

On a scale from 1 to 10, with 10 being very confident and 1 being not confident at all, how confident are you that you can change your alcohol and/or drug use?

Berg and Miller call this a scaling question and use it to help their clients determine whether they think they actually have the ability to change. After asking this question, Berg and Miller often follow up with:

What would have to happen for you to move up one number on the scale?

This helps to determine what types of conditions must be met or changes made to slightly improve the likelihood that change will occur. This question also helps to determine what the first steps in the change process will be. Use Worksheet 4 to answer these questions for yourself. Reading the example below before you complete Worksheet 4 may be helpful.

Example: Lloyd decided that he was ready to quit using cocaine. He had been a longtime user of cocaine and had tried unsuccessfully before to quit using. Therefore, he was not all that confident that he could be successful. When asked about the scale from 1 to 10, Lloyd said he was at a 6. Lloyd then wondered what would have to happen for him to move up to a 7 on the scale. He decided that in order to reach 7 he would need his wife to stop yelling at him about his cocaine use and offer her support in his efforts to quit. Lloyd then went to his wife to talk to her about his thoughts.

HOW TO USE THE REST OF THIS BOOK

Up to this point you have done a lot of thinking about what you want to change and how you will go about changing it. To close out this chapter I'd like to offer some tips on how to successfully use the rest of this book. As mentioned at the beginning of this chapter, this book is appropriate for use by people seeking to manage AOD problems, treatment providers, and students in counselor programs. Each of these groups may find this book useful in different ways, and I have provided some suggestions for each group of readers below. It should be noted, however, that these are only suggestions. If you find a different and better way to work through the chapters in this book—do it! Do whatever works and share your successes with others.

Those Seeking Help

When I began thinking about writing this book, I had in mind as my target audience those people wanting to make a change to their patterns of AOD use. Although I began to think about how other groups such as treatment providers and counselors-in-training could use the book, I worked hard to maintain my focus on providing a resource for persons with AOD problems. Hopefully, these efforts will show through in the chapters that follow.

If you are seeking help for an AOD issue, I suggest that you work carefully through each chapter and activity in this book. Take as much time as you need on each part of the book and do not move on until you understand the content. You may even find it helpful to go through each chapter more than once. Your road to change is not a race and you won't get there overnight. So, take your time, let the information sink in, and practice what you learn. It may take you several attempts to get the full benefit from the material in this book, so don't give up if you are not immediately successful.

I want to emphasize that this book is not a cure-all or substitute for good counseling. If you have success with this book—*great!* You likely worked hard on the chapters and had a strong desire to change your habits. You are to be congratulated. However, your journey toward change may not be over with the completion of this book. If you find that you are having a hard time maintaining the changes you made, experiencing desires to use alcohol or drugs in problematic ways, or if others are expressing worry about your AOD use, you may want to seek professional help.

On the other hand, if you do not experience success with this book, do not give up. A lack of positive results does not mean that you didn't work hard or have a desire to change your AOD use habits. It is possible that the material presented in this book was just not for you. Different people benefit from different types of treatment, and some other forms of help may be better suited for you. Seek help from treatment providers—they can help you figure out what your next step should be. Again, do not give up!

Treatment Providers

Treatment providers may find this book to be useful in a variety of ways. The book can be used as a psychoeducational curriculum for group counseling, a structural outline for individual treatment, a complement to therapy (e.g., homework assignments, bibliotherapy, etc.), or in any other way you see fit. As you read through the content of this book, make sure you have a deep understanding of what is being presented before you use it to work with clients. Read the references provided at the end of this book and conduct regular literature reviews to enhance this program. It may also be helpful for you to come up with your own examples to illustrate the chapter concepts. This will increase the likelihood that you will provide effective services to the clients you serve.

Additionally, I urge you to personalize the content of this book to your work with clients. If you find that something from the book works well with your clients, do more of it. If something does not work, discontinue doing it. Think of this book as a guide for treatment instead of a strict step-by-step prescription. The more you individualize the content of this book to your therapeutic style and to the clients you serve, the more successful you will be.

Finally, many of the instruments used in this book, such as the SOCRATES and Readiness Ruler in Chapter 2, are available in the public domain. I recommend you use these and other research-based instruments with your clients as a way to assess treatment readiness and spark discussion. References for each of these instruments are provided at the end of the book, and they are readily available on the World Wide Web.

Counselors-in-Training

Last, but certainly not least, counselors-in-training may find the content of this book valuable to their training in a variety of ways. Very few texts on AOD treatment provide a hands-on, practical presentation for applying concepts in the field to actual practice. I have tried to bridge that gap with this book. However, I do not recommend that this book be used as a primary text for any training course on AOD treatment. Rather, this book should be used as a supplement to another conceptual or theoretical text on AOD treatment.

If used in conjunction with another text, this book can provide counselors-in-training with the opportunity to engage the material in a variety of ways. The same rules of learning discussed above for persons seeking help with AOD issues also apply to counselors-in-training. Therefore, using this book as part of a training program can encourage active learning through the use of concrete examples, opportunities for reflection, and the chance to engage in practice of new skills. Counselors-in-training may even find it helpful to run mock counseling groups using the material in this book as a way to practice service delivery. As with the other target populations for this book, I encourage counselors-in-training to use this text in any way they find helpful.

Worksheet 1: What Is It that I Want to Change?

One thing I want to change about my alcohol and drug use is:

_____

_____

_____

A second thing I want to change is:

_____

_____

_____

Third:

_____

_____

_____

Fourth:

_____

_____

_____

A final thing I want to change is:

_____

_____

_____

Worksheet 2: Top Five Reasons for Wanting to Change

People seek change for a variety of reasons. Some do it for family or friends, others do it to keep a job, and some do it for themselves. Why have you decided to change? Write down your top five reasons below and explain them in detail.

Reason 1

_____

_____

_____

Reason 2

_____

_____

_____

Reason 3

_____

_____

_____

Reason 4

_____

_____

_____

Reason 5

_____

_____

Worksheet 3: Decisional Balance Chart

My Reasons for Wanting to Change	My Reasons for Staying the Same

Source: This table was adapted from Miller, W. (2002). Enhancing motivation to change in substance abuse treatment: Treatment improvement protocol series, Tip 35. Rockville, MD: U.S. Department of Health and Human Services and is in the public domain.

Worksheet 4: Your Level of Confidence

On a scale from 1 to 10, with 10 being very confident and 1 being not confident at all, how confident are you that you can change your alcohol and/or drug use?

What number would you assign yourself on this scale? _____

Why? _____

_____

_____

_____

What would have to happen for you to move up one number on the scale? _____

1. _____

_____

_____

2. _____

_____

_____

3. _____

_____

_____

NOTES

2

THE CHANGE PROCESS

The first step in making change happen is to understand how change occurs. In this chapter you are going to learn a little bit about how people begin to change. You are also going learn about the word denial, which you probably have heard before. From studying the way that people change behaviors—everything from diet, exercise, and alcohol and drug use—scientists have found that people go through a five-step process when attempting to change something about themselves. You will learn about this in order to help you to get ready to make changes to your alcohol and other drug (AOD) use patterns. There are several structured activities and worksheets to complete during this chapter.

Before you begin working on this chapter think about the following questions. You may want to write some of your answers down on the "Notes" page at the end of this chapter.

1. Have heard the word denial? Where did you hear it? What do you think it means?
2. Has anyone ever told you that you were or are in denial? How did it feel to hear this? Did you believe them? Why or why not?
3. Have you ever successfully changed a behavior in the past—including alcohol and drug use? How did you do it? How long did it take you? Were you successful the first time you tried it?

READINESS FOR CHANGE

Now it's time to get started. You will begin this chapter by learning a little bit about your willingness and readiness to change your alcohol and drug use. Use the "Readiness Ruler" at the end of this chapter to help you accomplish this goal. Answer the questions on the "Readiness Ruler." Remember to answer honestly and make notes as you go along.

Questions for Thought

1. After taking an honest look at your readiness to change, what are your reactions?
2. Were you surprised by the ways you answered the questions?
3. How committed do you think you are to making changes to your patterns of AOD use?

CATEGORIES OF HELP SEEKERS

Another way to assess your readiness to change is to determine who has a problem with your AOD use and whose responsibility you think it is to make change happen. Berg and Miller (1995) describe three categories of people who present to treatment for AOD use problems. These are *complainants*, *visitors*, and *customers*. Complainants are best described as those who believe that other people, not themselves, have a problem with their AOD use. When complainants actually say that they want to change, they will only put forth a minimum amount of energy to make that change occur.

Example: Rich came to a counseling center for an assessment. He said that he may have been drinking too much lately but that it is not really his fault. Rich stated that if only his wife would stop nagging him he would not drink so much. Rich says that his wife should be in counseling instead of him because she is the one with the problem.

Visitors are those people who deny that they have a problem with AOD use at all and, therefore, see no need for themselves change. Visitors often put no effort into making change happen.

Example: Karen bought a self-help book on the topic of alcoholism. She only bought the book, however, because her mother insisted that she do something about her drinking. Karen thought her mother was overreacting and believed that if her mother saw the book laying around the house she may stop talking about alcohol all the time.

Finally, customers are those people who recognize that there is a problem and acknowledge that the solution to the problem will require their contribution to bring about resolution.

Example: Jason realized he had a problem with cocaine after he spent his last dollar on getting high. He talked with his girlfriend about the problem, researched help on the Internet, and made an appointment with a counselor to discuss his options.

Think about these three groups as you progress through the rest of this chapter.

Questions for Thought

1. Are you a complainant, visitor, or customer?
2. What was your motivation for buying this book?
3. Is there anyone else besides yourself who will need to make changes in order for you to be successful?

DENIAL

Now that you have started to think about your willingness to change, let's consider the word denial. As mentioned above, you may be familiar with the word denial and what it means. In fact, someone in your life may have even referred to you as being in denial at some point in your life. Start by reading and thinking about the following definition. As you read, reflect on the characteristics described in the definition and whether or not they sound like something you have experienced.

Definition of Denial

Denial is a disregard for reality. It is a form of unconscious self-deception—that is, when individuals are in denial when they are not aware that they are deceiving themselves about problems they are experiencing (for example, "I have my drug use under control. I don't have a problem"). Denial allows a person to trick himself or herself into thinking everything is okay.

People in denial often say that they don't have a problem and see no negative consequences of AOD use. When others tell them they have a problem, they deny it and place blame for their actions on other people or things. Likewise, negative consequences of alcohol and drug use are seen as being the fault of some other person (for example, "My boss was just out to get me when he fired me for being late"). People in denial are said to have "tunnel vision." Negative consequences related to use are often described as: (a) someone else's problem, (b) a misunderstanding, (c) being in the wrong place at the wrong time, and (d) someone being "out to get" the alcohol or drug user.

In addition to the above, people in denial see positive aspects of alcohol and drug use (e.g., fun, being high, temporary relief of problems) and don't recognize and accept the bad consequences as being their fault (e.g., relationship problems, financial problems, legal problems). The most important point about denial is that the person denies having a problem in the face of several negative consequences of their behavior. To summarize:

- The person in denial is either unaware of or actively denies a problem.
- The person in denial places blame on others for any negative consequences.
- Denial is used to reduce anxiety about personal behaviors that lead to problems.

Questions for Thought

1. Can you think of a time when a friend or a family member was in denial of a problem?
2. What kinds of things were they saying about the problem?
3. How did they react when the problem was discussed?
4. Now that you know more about the concept of denial, can you think of a time when you may have been in denial of a problem?
5. If yes, how did you feel when others brought the problem up?

THE PROCESS OF CHANGE

Now that you know a little about denial it is time to learn about the steps or stages that people go through when they make changes in their lives. Scientists and researchers have been studying change for years. They have studied how people make changes in their diet, how they make changes to comply with doctors orders to take medication, and even how people follow through on their New Year's Eve resolutions. In the past several years, these researchers have begun to study how people make changes to behaviors related to alcohol and drug use. They have discovered that change is a five-step process, known as the *stages of change*.

The Stages of Change

There are five stages that people go through when changing behavior, particularly alcohol and drug use. What this means is that people go through a series of five steps when changing habits and lifestyles. These stages are outlined below (they are adapted from Connors, Donovan, and DiClemente, 2000). As you read about the stages of change it may be helpful to refer to "The Stages of Change" diagram at the end of this chapter. This diagram represents the stages of change on a wheel to demonstrate how the change process occurs.

Stage 1: I don't have a problem (denial). In this stage people are unaware of a problem or aware of a problem with no desire to change it. If they are aware of a problem, they see more pros than cons to continuing to engage in the problem behavior. When people are in this stage, they are often told that they are in denial of a problem or are resistant to making changes. People in this stage do not seek treatment on their own and will only do so if required by someone else. They may be defensive when discussing the problem and see it as someone else's problem rather than their own.

Example: John was referred to treatment for his third drunk driving offense. He states that he does not have a problem with alcohol because he only drinks beer. He also says he can quit drinking any time. He believes that his legal problems are the result of being in the wrong place at the wrong time and being labeled a trouble maker by law enforcement in his town.

Stage 2: thinking about change—I need to, I don't need to. In the second stage of change, people begin to think that it might be possible that a problem exists. They might begin thinking about making a change but have not yet made any attempts. At times, people in this stage think they might have a problem, and at other times they think they don't have a problem. People in this stage begin to weigh the pros and cons of their behavior and start thinking seriously about making changes. This is the first real step in the change process.

Example: After taking part in treatment for 4 weeks, John begins to wonder whether he might have a problem with alcohol. He starts to weigh the pros and cons of drinking and for the first time in his life the thought of quitting crosses his mind. On other days, however, John thinks he is starting to go crazy and that the counselors are just manipulating him into thinking he has a problem. He is spending many sleepless nights wondering whether or not he has a problem with alcohol and what he can do about it.

Stage 3: making a plan to change. The third stage of the change process is the planning stage. In this stage, people have acknowledged the fact that they may have a problem and are beginning to form plans to change their behavior. They may begin to take small steps toward change but are really only committed to coming up with ideas at this point. These people are on the verge of making changes in behavior and are ready to commit.

Example: John has finally decided that he has a problem with alcohol. With the help of his counselor and peers in group counseling he is developing a plan to stop drinking.

Stage 4: taking action to change. In the taking action stage, the fourth stage of change, people have started to put their plan into motion. They are making active attempts to change their behaviors. When people are in the action stage, their friends and loved ones notice differences in them. They have made changes to their lifestyle and are taking part in activities besides using drugs and alcohol.

Example: After John developed his plan, he began to make changes. He found a job that he liked, joined a basketball league, and stopped hanging out at the bars with his drinking friends. His wife and kids notice something different about him and tell him that they are proud of him.

Stage 5: keeping the change permanent. In the final stage people work to maintain changes they made in the action stage. They commit to leading a new lifestyle, continue to stick to their change plan, and take part in new and interesting activities as they move on with their lives. The changes that they made in the taking action stage have "stuck." People in this stage of change have made lasting changes to their lifestyle.

Example: John has been alcohol free for 2 years. He attends AA meetings, shows up ready to work and works hard every day, and spends lots of time with his family. In addition, John began coaching little league baseball in the summer, something he enjoyed when he was a kid. He also started learning to fix cars and is thinking about going to school to learn more about it.

Lapses. A final piece of the change process, as shown on the diagram, is lapses or relapses. It is not easy to quit using drugs and alcohol. Sometimes, even after several months or years of not using, people return briefly to alcohol or drug use. We call these lapses or relapses. When this happens, it is not the end of the world. It just means that people need to cycle through the change process again. For example, it usually takes smokers from three to seven cycles around the wheel to quit smoking. After a lapse, people intending to change must reevaluate their plan, make alterations to it, and put the new plan into action.

Example: After being clean for 2 years, John finds himself driving by his old bars. One day, he decides to stop in and see his old buddies. Before long, he is drinking a beer. That night, he does not return home until 2:30 in the morning and misses work the next day. John's wife and AA sponsor ask him what happened. He says "nothing" and tells them to stay out of his business. After several weeks of these questions, John starts to think that he might have a problem again. He revises his plan and puts it into action.

Now that you know a bit about the change process it may be helpful to fill out the "Personal Drug Use Questionnaire" at the end of this chapter. There is also a scoring sheet and instructions attached to the questionnaire. Complete this as well. Your answers to this questionnaire will help you to determine where you are in the change process.

Questions for Thought

1. What are your reactions to the questions you answered?
2. What stage of change did the questionnaire indicate you are in?

3. Do you think the results were accurate?

VALUES AND CHANGE

When people reach the stage of "keeping the change permanent," they have made significant changes to their personal beliefs and values. Beliefs are something accepted as true, especially an idea or set of ideas about how a person is to behave or act as part of his or her culture.

Values are beliefs in which there is an emotional investment. Values are ideas we have about what is good and what is bad and how things should be. We have values about family relationships (e.g., the role of the husband, wife, and children), about work relationships (e.g., how employers should treat employees), and about other personal and relationship issues (e.g., how children should behave toward adults, or how people should follow particular religious beliefs).

Oftentimes, people with a history of problematic AOD use experience times when their values differ from those around them. These are called value differences and are important to the change process. Value differences are those differences in people's fundamental beliefs about what is good and bad, right and wrong. When people's values differ significantly the resulting conflict is often very hard to resolve. Oftentimes, people are not willing to change or compromise their fundamental values and beliefs.

In order to make change stick, the person working on change has to address these value differences. For example, society says that it is wrong to steal from other people, no matter what the reason. The alcohol or drug abuser, however, may have a different value system that says stealing is okay under certain circumstances. In order to live a crime-free lifestyle alcohol and drug abusers that steal must change their values to be more in line with those values held by the majority of people in their culture—namely, that stealing is wrong.

Questions for Thought

1. What values do you hold that are different from other people in your life?
2. Have these value differences ever caused any problems in your life?

DETERMINING MY VALUES

The first step in changing values, addressing value differences, and "keeping the change permanent" is to assess your current values. To simplify things, values can be described as anti-social or pro-social.

Anti-Social Values

Anti-social values show a disregard for the rights of others, rules and laws, and disrespect of society in general. They are "me first" values; a person with this set of values does not consider the needs and rights of others to be important.

Anti-social values can lead to unlawful behaviors, deceitfulness, irresponsibility, and lack of remorse for hurting others. Sometimes, but not always, a person who has a history of AOD abuse has at least a few values that can be described as anti-social. Using and selling drugs, stealing and conning others, and assaulting others are just a few examples of things a person might do while actively abusing AOD.

Pro-Social Values

Pro-social values show respect for others and self, contribute to the good of society—or at least do not cause harm—and demonstrate a commitment to follow rules and laws of society. Pro-social values are "everyone is important" values; a person with this set of values takes all people's needs and rights into account before making decisions. Pro-social values are usually associated with the following areas (Hazelden, 2002):

1. *Security*—feeling secure about the future.
2. *Influence*—having my opinions respected by others.
3. *Achievement*—feeling like I have accomplished something.
4. *Health*—taking good care of my body and mind.
5. *Work*—contributing by being a good worker; making sure the work I do is first rate.
6. *Recognition*—being noticed and respected for who I am.
7. *Helpfulness*—enjoying the opportunity to help others when they need and ask for it.
8. *Freedom*—being free to do as I wish as long as it does not harm or disrespect other people.
9. *Friendliness*—caring about other people and being a trustworthy friend, coworker, employee, and acquaintance.
10. *Family*—valuing and respecting those close to me and letting them know this.
11. *Orderliness*—being organized in a way that lets me get things done that need to get done.

Worksheet 1, which was adapted from Hazelden (2002), will assist you in determining your values. Answer the questions on the worksheet and reflect on your responses.

Questions for Thought

1. What did you learn about your values by completing Worksheet 1?
2. Did your answers surprise you?
3. What values do you think it will be most important for you to change as you work through this book?

Sorting the Anti-Social from the Pro-Social

To finish this chapter it should be said that assessing your values is not always a simple task. Sometimes it is easy to figure out those values that are anti-social and those that are pro-social. Other times it is not. To illustrate this, read the scenario below and think about the questions for thought that follow. This scenario is a variation of Lawrence Kohlberg's classic "Hans Dilemma."

John's wife has been diagnosed with cancer and has been told that she has 3 weeks to live. However, a new drug has been developed that can cure the type of cancer that John's wife has. The catch is that the new drug is very expensive. Because John does not have health insurance or enough money to pay for the drug, he is unable to get the medicine that his wife needs.

John offers to pay a pharmacist at a later date or work out a payment plan to obtain the drug. The pharmacist refuses. So, one night John breaks into the pharmacy, steals the new drug, and gives it to his wife. Two days later she is cured.

Questions for Thought

1. Do you think that John did the right thing? Why or why not?

2. Did he demonstrate anti-social values? Pro-social values?

3. Is there a right or wrong answer to this dilemma?

4. What else could John have done?

5. Do you think the pharmacist was right to deny John a way to get the new drug? Why or why not?

6. What would you have done in this situation? Why?

SUMMARY

In this chapter you learned about the concepts of readiness for change and denial. You also learned about the steps that a person goes through when making a change and the need to alter some of your values to make changes "stick." However, insight and knowledge alone do not make change happen; it is what you do with the information that is important. So, now that you understand how change happens it is time to get to work! To finish the chapter use Worksheet 2 to identify one specific problem that you want to change. Use your completed worksheets from the previous chapter to help you with this. You will refer back to this problem later in the book. In the next chapter you will learn about one key element of making changes to your AOD use; how you think.

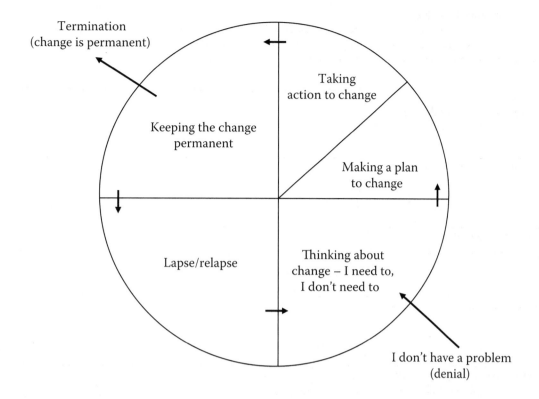

The Stages of Change Model *This diagram was adapted from Miller, W. (2002).* Enhancing motivation to change in substance abuse treatment: Treatment improvement protocol series, Tip 35. *Rockville, MD: U.S. Department of Health and Human Services and is in the public domain.*

Worksheet 1: Clarifying My Values

Read each value below. In the space provided rate each value as: 1. "*important,*" 2. "*not important,*" or 3. "*I have never thought about it.*" Then provide an example of some things that you have done that are either consistent or different from this value. Behaviors that are consistent are *pro-social* behaviors. Behaviors that are different are *anti-social* behaviors.

Value	Importance to me	Example of behavior consistent or different from this value
Security: feeling secure about the future		
Influence: having my opinions respected by others		
Achievement: feeling like I have accomplished something		
Health: taking good care of my body and mind		
Work: contributing by being a good worker; making sure the work I do it first rate		
Recognition: being noticed and respected for who I am		
Helpfulness: enjoying the opportunity to help others when they need and ask for it		
Freedom: being free to do as I wish as long as it does not harm or disrespect other people		
Friendliness: caring about other people and being a trustworthy friend, coworker, employee, and acquaintance.		
Family: valuing and respecting those close to me and letting them know this		
Orderliness: being organized in a way that lets me get things done that need to get done		

Source: Adapted from information provided in: Hazelden, (2002). Socialization: A cognitive behavioral treatment curriculum. Center City, MN: Hazelden Press.

Worksheet 2

To finish this chapter you will identify a behavior that you would like to change that is related to your goals in Chapter 1. This behavior can but does not have to be related to alcohol or drug use. Explain the problem and identify at least 3 steps you can take to change it.

Problem: _____

_____

_____

_____

Step 1: _____

_____

_____

_____

Step 2: _____

_____

_____

_____

Step 3: _____

_____

_____

_____

Readiness Ruler: CASAA Research Division

Using the ruler show below, indicate how ready you are to make a change (quit or cut down) in your use of the drugs shown. If you are *not at all* ready to make a change, you would circle the 1. If you are already trying hard to make a change, you would circle 10. If you are unsure whether you want to make a change, you would circle 3, 4, or 5. If you don't use a type of drug, circle "don't use" in the box at the right.

Circle one answer for each type of drug

Types of drugs	Not ready to change		Unsure		Ready to change			Trying to change		or: I don't use of this type of drug
	1 2	3	4	5	6 7	8	9	10		
Alcohol	1 2	3	4	5	6 7	8	9	10		Don't use
Tobacco	1 2	3	4	5	6 7	8	9	10		Don't use
Marijuana/ cannabis	1 2	3	4	5	6 7	8	9	10		Don't use
Tranquilizers	1 2	3	4	5	6 7	8	9	10		Don't use
Sedatives/ downers	1 2	3	4	5	6 7	8	9	10		Don't use
Steroids	1 2	3	4	5	6 7	8	9	10		Don't use
Stimulants/ uppers	1 2	3	4	5	6 7	8	9	10		Don't use
Cocaine	1 2	3	4	5	6 7	8	9	10		Don't use
Hallucinogens	1 2	3	4	5	6 7	8	9	10		Don't use
Opiates	1 2	3	4	5	6 7	8	9	10		Don't use
Inhalants	1 2	3	4	5	6 7	8	9	10		Don't use
Other drugs	1 2	3	4	5	6 7	8	9	10		Don't use
	Not ready to change		Unsure		Ready to change			Trying to change		
	1 2	3	4	5	6 7	8	9	10		

Source: This instrument was accessed at http://casaa.unm.edu/ and is available in the public domain.

Personal Drug Use Questionnaire: (SOCRATES 8D)—CASAA Research Division

Please read the following statements carefully. Each one describes a way that you might (or might not) feel *about your drug use*. For each statement, circle one number from 1 to 5, to indicate how much you agree or disagree with it *right now*. Please circle one and only one number for every statement.

	No! Strongly disagree	No Disagree	? Undecided or unsure	Yes Agree	Yes! Strongly agree
1. I really want to make changes in my use of drugs.	1	2	3	4	5
2. Sometimes I wonder if I am an addict.	1	2	3	4	5
3. If I don't change my drug use soon, my problems are going to get worse.	1	2	3	4	5
4. I have already started making some changes in my use of drugs.	1	2	3	4	5
5. I was using drugs too much at one time, but I've managed to change that.	1	2	3	4	5
6. Sometimes I wonder if my drug use is hurting other people.	1	2	3	4	5
7. I have a drug problem.	1	2	3	4	5
8. I'm not just thinking about changing my drug use, I'm already doing something about it.	1	2	3	4	5
9. I have already changed my drug use, and I am looking for ways to keep from slipping back to my old pattern.	1	2	3	4	5
10. I have serious problem with drugs.	1	2	3	4	5
11. Sometimes I wonder if I am in control of my drug use.	1	2	3	4	5
12. My drug use is causing a lot of harm.	1	2	3	4	5
13. I am actively doing things now to cut down or stop my use of drugs.	1	2	3	4	5
14. I want help to keep from going back to the drug problems that I had before.	1	2	3	4	5
15. I know that I have a drug problem.	1	2	3	4	5
16. There are times when I wonder if I use drugs too much.	1	2	3	4	5
17. I am a drug addict.	1	2	3	4	5
18. I am working hard to chage my grug use.	1	2	3	4	5
19. I have made some changes in my drug use, and I want some help to keep from going back to the way I used before.	1	2	3	4	5

Source: This instrument was taken from Miller, W. (2002). Enhancing motivation to change in substance abuse treatment: Treatment improvement protocol series, Tip 35. *Rockville, MD: U.S. Department of Health and Human Services and is in the public domain.*

SOCRATES–8D SCORING SHEET

Recognition	Ambivalence	Taking steps
1_____		
	2_____	
3_____		
		4_____
		5_____
	6_____	
7_____		
		8_____
		9_____
10_____		
	11_____	
12_____		
		13_____
		14_____
15_____		
	16_____	
17_____		
		18_____
		19_____
_____	_____	_____
Recognition	Ambivalence	Taking seps

Recognition + Ambivalence + Taking seps = _____
Total socrates score

INSTRUCTIONS: For each item, copy the circled number from the answer sheet next to the item above. Then sum each column to calculate scale totals. Sum these totals to calculate the total socrates score.

SOCRATE Profile Sheet *From the SOCRATES scoring form (19-item version) transfer the total scale scores into the empty boxes at the bottom of the Profile Sheet. Then for each scale, CIRCLE the same value above it to determine the decile range.*

Decile scores	Recognition	Ambivalence	Taking steps
90 Very high		19–20	39–40
80		18	37–38
70 High	35	17	36
60	34	16	34–35
50 Medium	32–33	15	33
40	31	14	31–32
30 Low	29–30	12–13	30
20	27–28	9–11	26–29
10 Very low	7–26	4–8	8–25
Raw scores (from scoring sheet)	Re=	Am=	Ts=

Guidelines for Interpretation of SOCRATES-8 Scores *Using the SOCRATES Profile Sheet, circle the client's raw score within each of the three scale columns. This provides information as to whether the client's scores are low, average, or high relative to people already seeking treatment for alcohol problems. The following are provided as general guidelines for interpretation of scores, but it is wise in an individual case also to examine individual item responses for additional information.*

RECOGNITION

HIGH scorers directly acknowledge that they are having problems related to their drinking, tending to express a desire for change to perceive that harm will continue if they do not change.

LOW scorers deny that alcohol is causing them serious problems, reject diagnostic labels such as "problem drinker" and "alcoholic," and do not express a desire for change.

AMBIVALENCE

HIGH scorers say that they sometimes *wonder* if they are in control of their drinking, are drinking too much, are hurting other people, and/or are alcoholic. Thus a high score reflects ambivalence or uncertainty. A high score here reflects some openness to reflection, as might be particularly expected in the contemplation stage of change.

LOW scorers say that they *do not wonder* whether they drink too much, are in control, are hurting others, or are alcoholic. Note that a person may score low on ambivalence *either* because they "know" their drinking is causing problems (high Recognition), or because they "know" that they do not have drinking problems (low Recognition). Thus a low Ambivalence score should be interpreted in relation to the Recognition score.

TAKING STEPS

HIGH scorers report that they are already doing things to make positive change in their drinking, and may have experienced some success in this regard. Change is under way, and they may want help to persist or to prevent backsliding. A high score on this scale has been found to be predictive of successful change.

LOW scorers report that they are not currently doing things to change their drinking and have not made such changes recently.

NOTES

_____

_____

_____

_____

_____

_____

_____

_____

_____

_____

_____

_____

_____

_____

3

COGNITIVE-BEHAVIORAL MODEL OF ADDICTION

In this chapter you will learn about cognitive-behavioral theory of alcohol and other drug (AOD) abuse. Alcohol and drug abuse treatment that uses the cognitive-behavioral model of addiction is called cognitive-behavioral therapy, or CBT. CBT was created by the pioneering researchers and scientists Dr. Albert Ellis (2001) and Dr. Aaron Beck and colleagues (2001). CBT is the theory that our behaviors and feelings are influenced by the way we think. This means that in order to change what you do and how you feel, you have to change the way you think about situations. CBT is used in a lot of different settings as treatment for alcohol and drug abuse. Research has shown it to be highly effective, that it works. Although CBT may not explain every aspect of AOD abuse, most researchers and treatment providers would agree that changing the way you think is one of the most important steps in successfully changing AOD use patterns. Chances are that if you enter into substance abuse treatment, you will experience CBT.

The purpose of this chapter is to introduce you to the cognitive-behavioral model of AOD abuse. By the end of the chapter, you should:

1. Understand the basic ideas of the cognitive-behavioral model.
2. Understand the relationship between thoughts, behaviors, and feeling.
3. Understand how thoughts and previous experiences influence alcohol and drug abuse.
4. Be able to identify how appraisals, beliefs, and attributions are related to alcohol and drug abuse.
5. Be able to use the Strategic Thinking Model to analyze past and present behaviors.

You may find that the information presented in this chapter is difficult to learn. If so, review the chapter several times and work through the examples. Understanding CBT will be an important step in learning to change alcohol and drug abuse problems.

COGNITIVE-BEHAVIORAL THEORY

Cognitive-behavioral theory teaches us that the way a person thinks will influence the way he or she feels and behaves. The theory says that thoughts lead to behaviors. One cannot do something or take some sort of action without first thinking about it. For example, a person does not respond to a verbal threat without first having some thought about the threat. Different people have different thoughts and beliefs. This is why different people react differently in certain situations. This is also why different people behave differently. The following example demonstrates this concept.

Example: Jennifer and Lauren were both late to work. Their supervisor noticed that they were late and gave them a verbal warning about their tardiness. Jennifer thought her supervisor was being unreasonable and should have let her slide. As a result, she became angry and was unproductive at work for the rest of the day. Lauren, on the other hand, believed that being late to work was wrong and demonstrated a poor work ethic. As a result, she was embarrassed that she was late and apologized several times to her supervisor. She also attempted to hide from her coworkers on breaks and lunch for fear that they would have negative ideas about her.

Learning

Cognitive-behavioral theory states that thoughts and behaviors are learned. Because alcohol and drug abuse is a behavior, it is considered to be *learned* activity. Alcohol and drug use is a result of maladaptive thought processes. Since these thoughts and behaviors are learned, they can also be *unlearned*.

Sources of Learning

Learning occurs through multiple sources. These are:

1. Behaviors that are rewarded are repeated. When a behavior is rewarded frequently during early instances, it is more likely to "stick." As a result, when negative problems begin to occur as a result of the behavior, it is harder to change because of strong beliefs that the behavior will cause "positive" effects.
2. Behaviors that are not rewarded are usually not repeated. For example, if a person loses a large amount of money the first time he gambles, he is less likely to gamble again.
3. People are likely to engage in behaviors that they see other important people in their lives doing. If a person is brought up in a family where marijuana use is a frequent occurrence, that person is more likely to smoke marijuana. Likewise, if a person notices that a local drug dealer has nice possessions and the "respect" of others in the neighborhood, he or she may be more likely to want to deal drugs, too.
4. A person is likely to engage in the same behaviors as their social group. For example, a person who associates with the top students in his or her high school class is also likely to get good grades. A person who associates with hard workers on the job is also likely to work hard. A person involved in a street gang is likely to engage in behaviors consistent with other gang members including violence, crime, and substance abuse.

Just as individuals learned to engage in problematic alcohol and drug use through the above processes, they can also "unlearn" these behaviors and learn new ones. This can be done when a person receives a positive outcome for some positive behavior. Behaviors can also be "unlearned" when a person begins to experience consistent negative outcomes for negative behaviors (e.g., frequent arrests for criminal behavior). Our thoughts, beliefs, and attitudes influence our actions and feelings. Therefore, in order to learn new behaviors and ways of relating to peoples, we must first change our thoughts.

THE A-B-C OF CHANGE

To understand how thoughts influence behaviors we often do what is called an A-B-C analysis. This is as follows:

A: stands for an activating event,
B: stands for our beliefs and thoughts about the event,
C: stands for the consequent behavior or feeling.

The sequence goes as follows:

A	$\rightarrow$	B	$\rightarrow$	C
Activating		Belief		Consequent
event		or thought		feeling/behavior

Functional Thoughts

Functional thoughts lead to functional behavior. For example, if a person thinks and believes that it is important to be a good parent, family member, and friend he or she will probably engage in behaviors that lead to positive interactions with those around him or her. Therefore, the person will be less likely to misuse drugs and alcohol or commit crimes.

Example: Max was referred to treatment for his third drunk driving offense. He states that he has a drinking problem and has been unable to control his use of alcohol. John believes that his legal problems are the result of his poor choices about alcohol use.

Dysfunctional Thoughts

Dysfunctional thoughts lead to dysfunctional behavior. For example, a person who thinks and believes that he or she deserves everything should be handed to him or her will be less likely to work hard for the things he or she wants. These types of thoughts, called errors in thinking, are discussed in the Chapter 4.

Example: Max was referred to treatment for his third drunk driving offense. He states that he does not have a problem with alcohol because he only drinks beer. He also says he can quit drinking any time. He believes that his legal problems are the result of being in the wrong place at the wrong time and being labeled a trouble maker by law enforcement in his town and states that he drives better when he is drunk.

Expectations, Appraisals, Attributions

When any type of situation occurs (*A* in the A-B-C analysis) our thoughts and beliefs are activated (*B*). Part of the thought process (*B* in the A-B-C analysis) involves the following:

Expectations: based on learning, rewards, and experience, we begin to have expectations about what is going to happen.

Example: Henry was pulled over by a police officer for speeding (*A* in the A-B-C analysis). Because he has numerous arrests he believes that the police are only out to hassle him, and generally thinks negatively about police officers (part of the *B* in the A-B-C). As a result of this expectation, Henry had a negative attitude when talking with the police officer and was eventually given several citations other than just a speeding ticket (e.g., he had something hanging from his rearview mirror).

Appraisals: when a situation occurs, a person judges or evaluates it automatically. These appraisals are also based on thoughts, beliefs, and past experience.

Example: In the same situation above, after Henry saw the lights on the police car indicating that he should pull over he quickly began to appraise the situation. Because he had several negative experiences with police officers in the past, Henry's appraisal of the situation was that he might be in some kind of trouble. As a result, Henry decided not to pull over and fled the police officer. He was eventually caught and arrested.

Attributions: when a situation occurs, a person attributes the cause of the situation to someone or something. The person may believe that the situation is the result of something he or she did, luck, or the actions of someone else.

Example: After being arrested for fleeing a police officer, Henry began to think about who was to blame for the mess that he was in. He attributed his problem to being hassled by the police and therefore placed blame on them for his behavior. Because the police were to blame, Henry told himself that he had no choice but to flee the police officer and therefore did nothing wrong.

Automatic Thoughts

Because expectations, appraisals, and attributions are based on previous experiences and long-held beliefs, they are often *automatic*. This means that the person spends little time thinking about what he or she expects to happen, how he or she appraises the situation, and who or what he or she attributes blame to. These processes happen quickly.

When applied to treatment of alcohol and drug abuse, CBT asks: What has happened in a person's life to get him or her to the point of substance misuse? What problems have resulted? Is change necessary? and If so, what thoughts and beliefs lead to problems? The goal of CBT counseling is to change the way a person thinks about a situation in order to change the way that person behaves. This involves changing the *B* part of the A-B-C of the situation.

Questions for Thought

1. Using the examples above of Henry being pulled over for speeding, how might the outcome of the situation have been different if Henry had different expectations for the situations?
2. How would different appraisals or attributions change the outcome?

STRATEGIC THINKING MODEL

The Strategic Thinking Model can assist a person in changing his or her dysfunctional and problematic thoughts. It is a tool that can analyze the way a person learned to react to situations and how that person can change reactions by changing his or her thoughts. The Strategic Thinking Model is a form of the A-B-C analysis described above. The model is shown in the "Strategic Thinking Model Flow Chart" at the end of this chapter. The flow chart shows how events lead to thoughts, which lead to actions, which lead to some sort of consequence.

The Strategic Thinking Model also shows how behaviors are learned. It demonstrates how behaviors are rewarded and how those rewards then influence our thoughts and beliefs. Therefore, it is important to highlight that for new behaviors to be learned, they must have some sort of positive reward. If they do not, the behavior will not be repeated. Applied to alcohol and drug abuse, a person must see the positives of refusing alcohol or drugs if the individual is to quit using them.

If you follow the flow chart from left to right you will see that the process of events to thoughts to behaviors to outcomes is described pictorially. Within each box, the A-B-Cs of the model are identified.

It is important to see on the flow chart that "bad" behaviors (e.g., alcohol and drug abuse) can have positive outcomes (relief from stress, quick money) and therefore will be repeated. It should also be noted that positive behaviors (e.g., signing up for school, attempting to reconnect with family) can have negative outcomes (e.g., failure) and therefore won't be repeated. In a nutshell, not all "good" behaviors are rewarded, and not all "bad" behaviors go unrewarded.

SUMMARY

In this chapter the basic ideas of cognitive-behavioral theory and the Strategic Thinking Model were outlined. The basic points are that our thoughts influence the way we think and act. In order to change what we do and how we feel, particularly as it relates to alcohol and drug abuse, we need to change the way that we think. In the next chapter we will learn more about the thinking patterns that can lead to alcohol and drug use. These are thinking errors and irrational beliefs.

There are two worksheets to complete in this chapter. The first asks you to continue thinking about the behaviors that you identified in Chapters 1 and 2 as wanting to change. The second worksheet asks you to walk through the Strategic Thinking Model with a personal example. If you experience difficulty with these worksheets, return to the chapter content and review the material. This is difficult stuff, so don't give up!

Worksheet 1

In Chapters 1 and 2 you identified goals and behaviors that you would like to change. Think about some dysfunctional thoughts that may be associated with the behaviors you identified and write them down. Then, identify some new, functional thoughts that may lead to your desired behavior change.

Dysfunctional Thoughts: _____

_____

_____

_____

_____

_____

Functional Thought 1: _____   *Functional Thought 2:* _____   *Functional Thought 3:* _____

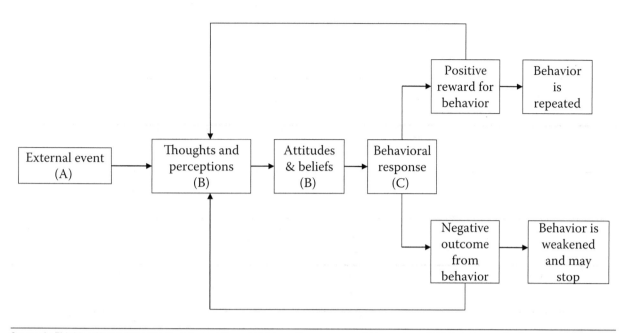

Strategic Thinking Model Flow Chart *Adapted from Michigan Department of Corrections (2001).* Advanced substance abuse treatment. *Lansing, MI: author.*

Worksheet 2

Using the chart below, identify a recent situation; your thoughts, perceptions, beliefs, and attitudes about the situation; and how you behaved. Identify the outcome. Was it positive or negative? If you changed your thoughts, beliefs, perceptions, or attitudes, how might you have reacted differently to the situation? Use the space provided in the boxes below.

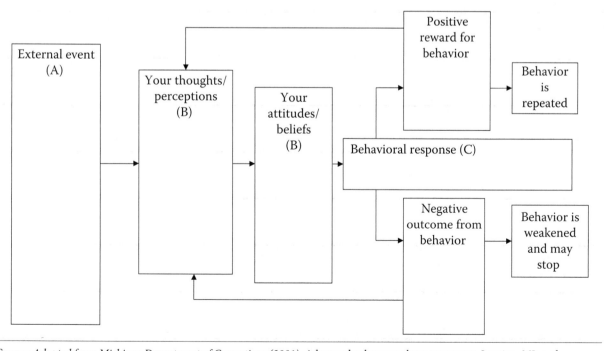

Source: Adapted from Michigan Department of Corrections (2001). Advanced substance abuse treatment. *Lansing, MI: author.*

NOTES

4

ERRORS IN THINKING

This chapter is a continuation of Chapter 3. In this chapter you will learn about problematic thoughts and beliefs that could lead to alcohol and drug abuse. These are called *thinking errors*. Errors in thinking occur in the *B* part of the A-B-C model. If you need to, go back and review Chapter 3 again; it will be important to understand that material before you work through this chapter. You will also learn more about functional thoughts in this chapter and how they can change behavior.

By the end of this chapter you should:

1. Understand errors in thinking and how they relate to alcohol and drug abuse.
2. Be able to identify errors in thinking by name and understand how they work.
3. Understand what functional thoughts are and how they relate to recovery from alcohol and drug problems.
4. Be able to identify how situations may have different outcomes due to changes in patterns of thinking (from thinking errors to functional thoughts).

Before you begin to work through this chapter check your reactions to the cognitive model of addiction.

1. Do you "buy" into what you learned in Chapter 3?
2. Have you started to look at your thinking patterns since reviewing Chapter 3?
3. How does the information you learned in Chapter 3 agree or disagree with information you learned in the past about alcohol and drug abuse?

Reviewing your reactions to these questions will be helpful as you work through the content of this chapter.

THINKING ERRORS

The term *thinking errors* describes problems in thinking that can lead to problems in behavior. Many scientists and researchers have tried to understand the problematic thoughts that occur in the *B* part of the A-B-C model and how those thoughts can lead to alcohol and drug abuse. Some of the leading researchers in this area are Dr. Albert Ellis (2001), Dr. Aaron Beck and his colleagues (2001), and Dr. Stanton Samenow (2004). These doctors have identified many thinking errors that are common to many persons with alcohol and drug abuse problems. In this part of the chapter, you will learn about several of these thinking errors and complete some activities that will help you to better understand this topic.

Many times, thinking errors are automatic (see Chapter 3 for a definition of automatic thoughts). Basically, automatic thoughts are those that are based on past experiences and just "pop into our heads" when evaluating a situation. Automatic thoughts direct our behavior without us even being aware of it. In treatment, you will learn how to slow down your thinking, confront automatic thinking errors, and establish more functional ways of thinking.

Listed below are several thinking errors that are common to people with alcohol and drug abuse problems. Review each of these and make sure you understand what they mean. This list is not meant to be all-inclusive. It only represents some common errors in thinking that people make.

1. *Arbitrary inference:* drawing a specific conclusion without evidence to support it. Arbitrary inference may occur when you assume that a person is treating you a certain way without any knowledge or evidence of his or her real motivations or intentions.

2. *Selective abstraction:* hearing only what you want to hear in a situation and ignoring other important information. For example, when being evaluated by a supervisor you may only hear the "negative" evaluations and ignore the positive ones. This may lead you to act or feel certain ways about your supervisor, self, and job.

3. *Overgeneralization:* seeing something as always happening even though it only has happened a few times. For example, you may overgeneralize that your child always ignores the rules of the house when in fact he or she follows them most of the time.

4. *Magnification/minimization:* seeing something as far more or less significant than it really is. An example of this thinking error is when you minimize your role in a problem at home and blame others for the problem.

5. *Personalization:* attributing external events to oneself. You may, for example, believe that your child's teacher has a negative opinion of you because the teacher disciplined your child for not doing his or her homework.

6. *Black and white thinking:* categorizing experience as either all good or all bad and oversimplifying a complex situation. For example, you may see yourself as worthless and unwanted after being turned down for one job.

7. *Quick fix thinking:* thinking that problems can be fixed quickly with minimal effort or maintenance activities ("I want what I want when I want it"). People sometimes think that they can overcome a drug and alcohol problem by simply moving away to a new place.

8. *Mustrabation:* "Things *must* go my way!" This thinking error happens when people have strong emotional reactions when things do not happen as they expect them to.

9. *Ego centric thinking:* this occurs when someone believes that what they say is the absolute truth, and what everyone else says is wrong.

10. *Catastrophizing:* making "mountains out of molehills" and blowing things out of proportion. You may, for instance, think a whole relationship is ruined because of one disagreement or argument.

11. *Victimization:* "I am not to blame for my situation." This is characterized by believing that others are to blame for what has happened to me or what I have done. A person with an alcohol or drug abuse problem, for instance, may blame that problem on a bad childhood.

12. *False pride:* overcompensating for feelings of inadequacy and poor self-esteem or using pride as an excuse for avoiding a task that makes one uncomfortable. A person recovering from alcohol or drug addiction may feel false pride when confronting his or her own wrong doings (e.g., "A real man doesn't have to apologize for messing up").

13. *Just desserts:* thinking that other people "had it coming." For example, you may find yourself thinking that someone else was asking to have his or her house broken into because the person left his or her windows unlocked after going to bed.

14. *Power thrust:* thinking that in order to get respect and what you want you must aggressively dominate others. This error occurs when people think that things will never go their way unless they take what they want.

15. *Anger:* thinking that if I just show them how angry this makes me then I'll get my way.

Thinking errors are rigid ways of thinking about situations. For example, in the error *black and white thinking*, the associated thoughts force a person to think that the situation is either all good or bad. In reality, no situation is completely good or completely bad; there are both good and bad aspects in almost any situation.

Questions for Thought

1. What are your reactions to reading about these thinking errors?
2. Can you think of a time when you watched someone else have any of these thinking errors?
3. How about yourself?
4. Can you see how these thinking errors may influence behavior?

FUNCTIONAL THOUGHTS

Thinking errors are considered rigid, while functional thoughts are considered flexible. Functional means that the thoughts work and lead to behaviors that maximize the potential for positive outcomes. When a person has functional thinking patterns, he or she is able to assess each situation as unique, instead of seeing every situation in the same way (as is done with thinking errors). Therefore, a person is able to see multiple perspectives, see all of his or her options, weigh the pros and cons of certain actions, and act in ways that minimize negative outcomes and maximize positive outcomes. But, it is a thinking error to assume that functional thinking will always result in positive outcomes—*there are no absolutes*!

One skill that can be used to develop functional thinking skills is a technique known as playing the tape forward. This technique involves stopping to evaluate the thoughts you are having, predicting the behavior that will result from those thoughts, and then predicting what the outcome will be of that behavior. The following example will help explain this idea.

Example: John is in a situation where he is offended by his manager's comments to him. Before responding, he stops briefly to analyze the thoughts he is having. He realizes that the first thought that popped into his head was, "My supervisor must respect me at all times (the error of *mustrabation*)." He then played the tape forward and could see himself making offensive comments back to his supervisor. This may then result in him losing his job. Instead, John decided on the following functional thought, "Maybe I took his comment wrong or maybe he is having a bad day. I can't assume that he meant to offend me. Maybe I will go ask him about it after I have calmed down." When he played the tape forward on this thought, he saw himself remaining in control of his behavior and keeping his job.

WORKSHEETS AND ACTIVITIES

To complete this chapter use Worksheets 1 through 4 to identify several thinking errors that you can recognize in yourself. Then identify any functional thoughts that can be used to replace those thinking errors. Be sure you understand the concepts before trying the exercises.

SUMMARY

In Chapter 3 and this chapter you learned about cognitive theory and errors in thinking. You learned how your thoughts can influence your behavior, including alcohol and drug abuse. You also learned that in order to change these behaviors, you must first change your thoughts. In the next chapter you will learn how these principles of cognitive-behavioral theory relate to the process of recovery from problematic alcohol and other drug use.

Worksheet 1: Errors in Thinking

Below some common errors in thinking are listed. This list is not meant to be all-inclusive. It only represents some common errors that people make in thinking. Read each error in thinking and the example below it. Come up with examples you have experienced for each error.

Arbitrary inference: drawing a specific conclusion with or without evidence to support it.

Example: *My parole agent doesn't care about me; he just wants to try to get me back in prison. How do I know? Because he made me wait a half an hour for my meeting with him today, that's how.*

Your example: _____

_____

Selective abstraction: hearing only what you want to hear in a situation and ignoring other important information.

Example: *I got my employment review today and they gave me a good rating instead of an excellent rating in two of the areas. They just don't value me as a worker—I'm gonna start looking for another job.*

Your example: _____

_____

_____

Overgeneralization: seeing something as always happening even though it only has happened a few times.

Example: *Telling others that your boss always singles you out for problems on the job even though he has only done so a couple of times. Ignoring the times that you and your boss have gotten along well.*

Your example: _____

_____

_____

Magnification/minimization: seeing something as far more or less significant than it really is.

Example: *So what if I get caught stealing this car. I've already done time in jail and I can do more without a problem. It doesn't matter.*

Your example: _____

_____

_____

Personalization: attributing external events to oneself.

Example: *They stopped offering overtime at work because they knew that I was going to be getting a lot of it next month.*

Your example: _____

_____

_____

Black and white thinking: categorizing experience as either all good or all bad. Oversimplifying a complex situation and classifying it in one extreme or another.

Example: *I can't stand this job. It's the worst place I have ever worked. I was 5 minutes late yesterday and the supervisor wanted to know why.*

Your example: _____

_____

_____

Quick fix thinking: thinking problems can be fixed quickly with minimal effort or maintenance activities. "I want what I want when I want it."

Example: *I just need to sell this dope for a couple of months to get on my feet. Then I'll get a job and stop making money illegally.*

Your example: _____

_____

_____

Mustrabation: things *must* go my way.

Example: *I can't believe that the cops pulled me over for no good reason. They must respect me or else.*

Your example: _____

_____

_____

Worksheet 1: Errors in Thinking (continued)

Ego centric thinking: what I say is the absolute truth, what everyone else says is wrong.

Example: *These substance abuse counselors don't know what they are talking about. I lived this stuff. I should be the one teaching this class.*

Your example: _____

_____

_____

Catastrophizing: making "mountains out of molehills." Blowing things out of proportion.

Example: *I'm going to be late for my meeting with my probation officer today. I might as well not report again because he is just going to send me to jail again.*

Your example: _____

_____

_____

Victimization: "I am not to blame for my situation." Believing that others are to blame for what has happened to me or what I have done.

Example: *Yeah, so what that I was drinking and driving. I can handle my liquor. I just happened to be at the wrong place at the wrong time when I got into that accident. Besides, the other person was driving like a jerk.*

Your example: _____

_____

_____

False pride: overcompensating for feelings of inadequacy and poor self-esteem or using pride as an excuse for avoiding a task that makes one uncomfortable.

Example: *Men just don't apologize to each other. So what if I did something wrong, I don't do all that "touchy feely" stuff.*

Your example: _____

_____

_____

Just desserts: thinking that other people "had it coming."

Example: *If he didn't want his car stolen then he would have locked it up. He just got what he deserved. He was asking for it by leaving an unlocked car on this street.*

Your example: _____

_____

_____

Power thrust: "In order to get respect and what I want I must aggressively dominate others."

Example: *If they won't give it to me, I'll just take it. I earned it and I'll just have to show them how serious I am about this. Once I do they'll never forget it, they'll never disrespect me again.*

Your example: _____

_____

_____

Anger: thinking that if I just show them how angry this makes me then I'll get my way.

Example: *This just makes me angry to no end. I can't believe that they want me to move to second shift. I'm mad as hell and I'm not gonna take it!*

Your example: _____

_____

_____

Worksheet 2: Errors in Thinking

Read each scenario below and answer the following questions:

1. Apply a thinking error to each scenario below and play the tape forward. What do they think would happen if they reacted using the thinking error?

2. Then apply a functional thought to each situation. Play the tape forward. What do they think would happen?

Scenario 1

Bob just started a new job a few weeks ago. A few of his coworkers invited him out for drinks after their shift. Bob is on probation and can't be in or around places that serve alcohol. Bob also knows that one of the guys who asked him to go to the bar is on probation and has a serious alcohol problem. Bob really wants to get in with a good group of people at work.

What should Bob do? _____

_____

_____

_____

_____

_____

_____

_____

Scenario 2

John got out of jail last month for drinking and driving. He is having trouble getting around town to put in job applications because he does not have a valid driver's license. He has a car in his driveway that his cousin kept up for him while he was locked up. The car looks and runs great. It also looks a lot more comfortable than the bike seat he has been sitting on for the past few weeks. John's probation officer is putting a lot of pressure on him to get a job but does not understand that it difficult to get around town.

What should John do? _____

_____

_____

_____

_____

_____

_____

Scenario 3

David got caught drinking last week and violated his probation. He truthfully only had two beers and was walking home from a friend's house when he was stopped by the police. To make a long story short, he was arrested when it was discovered that he was on probation. Now his probation officer has referred him to a 90-day residential substance abuse treatment program. He got out of jail today and is supposed to report to the program for treatment tomorrow. He also has two job interviews on that day and doesn't want to miss them.

What should David do? _____

_____

_____

_____

_____

_____

_____

_____

Worksheet 3: Thinking Error

Think about a past situation, a thinking error that you used to appraise the situation, your behavioral response, and the positive or negative outcome that happened. How did this help you to learn to use the thinking error?

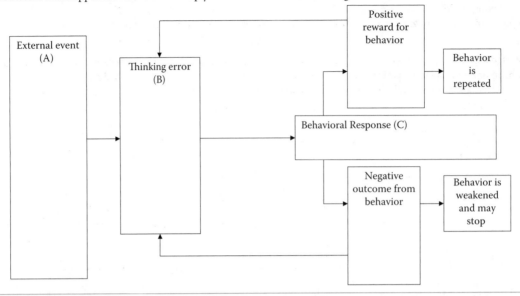

Source: Adapted from Michigan Department of Corrections (2001). Advanced substance abuse treatment. Lansing, MI: author.

Worksheet 4: Functional Thinking

Now think about a past situation, a functional thought that was used to appraise the situation, your behavioral response, and the positive or negative outcome that happened. How did this help you to learn to use functional thought?

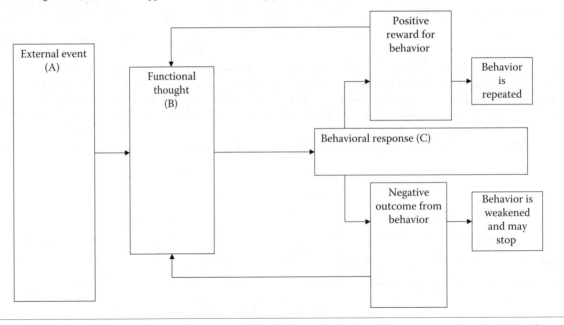

Source: Adapted from Michigan Department of Corrections (2001). Advanced substance abuse treatment. Lansing, MI: author.

NOTES

5

PATH TO RECOVERY

In this chapter you will learn about the process of recovery, a term you may be familiar with. You will begin to learn about controlling your alcohol and other drug (AOD) use and think about how you plan to live after you reach your goals. By the end of the chapter, you should be able to:

1. Define the term recovery.
2. Understand the developmental model of recovery.
3. Understand the "Wellness Wheel."
4. Identify areas of life that need to be improved.
5. Come up with a beginning plan to improve problem areas of your life.

WHAT IS RECOVERY?

Recovery is a term used in the substance abuse treatment field to indicate that a person is making active attempts to change his or her patterns of alcohol and drug use. It means that the person is abstaining from problematic alcohol and drug use and is developing a "full" biological, psychological, and social life. The person in recovery is truly in the action stage of change.

It is important to know that recovery is a day-to-day "process" rather than something that can be achieved over night. Some important points about recovery are listed below.

- Recovery is not an endpoint. You are never fully "recovered" from alcohol and drug addiction. Instead, you are "in recovery." This means that you are working toward a new lifestyle that does not involve problematic alcohol and drug use.
- You must work at your recovery every day. It is not something you can forget about.
- Recovery is something that happens because you want it to happen. It takes effort and desire. It is not something that someone else can give to you.
- Recovery is not always easy.
- Desires and urges to use alcohol and drugs may come and go. You must be aware of them and take action so you don't act on these desires and urges.

- Just because a person has an episode where he or she uses alcohol and drugs in a problematic way does not mean that that person is no longer in recovery. Instead it means the person had a "slip" or "relapse" (discussed more fully in the next chapter). A brief return to problematic alcohol and drug use may happen, but it does not have to continue. You can always return to the recovery lifestyle.
- You may find that associating with other people who are in recovery is helpful to you in your recovery.
- Recovery is to be taken one day at a time. It would be overwhelming to think about changing a behavior for the rest of your life. You can, however, manage to change a behavior for a single day. It has been suggested that in recovery you should worry about tomorrow when tomorrow comes.
- Recovery does not just involve changing your alcohol and drug use patterns. It involves changing many aspects of your life so that you may live in healthier and more productive ways. In recovery, changing your AOD use patterns is only the first step. In order to truly be in recovery, you must determine what you are going to do instead of using AOD in problematic ways.
- You may enter a "stuck point" in recovery. A stuck point happens when you stop making progress toward a better, healthier life. Simply put, you feel stuck. Stuck points are usually the result of a lack of confidence or ability to handle a stressful situation (U.S. Department of Health and Human Services, 2004). If this is not fixed, a stuck point could result in a slip or relapse.

THE DEVELOPMENTAL MODEL OF RECOVERY

The process of recovery can be divided into stages. This means that people go through different stages, set different goals, and confront different problems the longer they are in recovery. The stages of recovery are:

1. *Transition Stage:* In the transition period of recovery a person has his or her first experience with problems related to uncontrollable alcohol and drug use. During this stage, the person begins several unsuccessful attempts to cut down on alcohol and drug use.

2. *Stabilization Period:* During the stabilization period the person has determined that he or she has a problem with alcohol and drugs and must totally quit using the drug of choice. This stage involves detoxifying from alcohol and drugs and learning to break the psychological urges and desires to use. The person must stabilize his or her life.

3. *Early Recovery:* In early recovery, the person begins to establish an alcohol- and drug-free lifestyle. A major task involves separating from old friends who use alcohol and drugs and finding new places to go and new things to do. The person must also begin to develop thoughts, beliefs, and values that are associated with recovery. In early recovery the person should begin to think about alternative things and activities to do rather than the old things that he or she used to do when using AOD.

4. *Middle Recovery:* Middle recovery involves developing a balanced lifestyle. People in this stage begin to make amends with people they have hurt and repair the damage done in their lives. A balance between work, family, and recreation must be established.

5. *Late Recovery:* In late recovery, major changes are made to the personality. These changes involve going from personality issues that interfere with life satisfaction to those that enhance life satisfaction. People in late recovery have the ability to confront traumatizing experiences from their past including emotional, physical, and sexual abuse, abandonment, and poor parental care.

6. *Maintenance Stage:* Maintenance means that the person works to maintain the changes made in recovery and continues to grow and change as a person.

One of the main points is that as a person continues in recovery, his or her personal goals should change. For example, in the stabilization period the person is just trying to regain control of his or her life. In the middle recovery stage the person is trying to balance his or her life with work, family, and recreation. In other words, the person should develop different goals for different points of recovery.

Questions for Thought

1. Where are you in the process of recovery? What stage?
2. How do you think this model fits with the stages of change discussed in Chapter 2? Do you see similarities?

PLANNING FOR RECOVERY

Now that you have a basic understanding of recovery it is now time to think about the type of healthy, recovering lifestyle you want to lead. I can't stress enough that recovery is not just about changing your patterns of AOD use; it is also about developing healthier lifestyle alternatives. A healthy lifestyle is one that is balanced and leads to satisfaction in a variety of areas. The "Wellness Wheel," developed by Sharon Wegschieder-Cruse (1989), is one tool to help you create a plan for developing an emotionally healthy and well-balanced life.

The "Wellness Wheel" identifies seven areas of our daily lives that, if attended to, can lead to success in recovery. If each of these areas of life is attended to, a person is said to have a well-balanced, healthy life. If several of these areas are ignored, it will likely lead to dissatisfaction with life and a general sense that "something is missing." The seven areas of life identified on the "Wellness Wheel" are listed and discussed below.

Career

Satisfaction in your career can involve many aspects of your work. For example, you may feel satisfied in this area if you believe that you are valued at your workplace. Strong recovery in this area may also involve feelings of comfort and confidence in the workplace and feeling that your current job is meeting your goals for work. For example, you may ask yourself, "Is getting a paycheck my main goal for working or do I also need to get some other sort of satisfaction from my work?" It is not uncommon for persons with a history of alcohol and drug abuse to have a poor work history and little work experience.

Mental

Healthy mental recovery happens when you feel stimulated and challenged on a regular basis. Satisfaction in this area may come from engaging in creative and stimulating activities such as reading, playing chess, or completing projects around the house. Mental recovery involves using the resources around you to increase your knowledge about different things, develop new skills, and enhance your abilities. Oftentimes heavy alcohol and drug use discourages mental development.

Physical

Physical recovery involves maintaining a healthy body and lifestyle. Oftentimes those with a history of addiction have taken substances that are bad for their health and stopped taking part in physically challenging activities. Satisfaction in this area comes from taking part in healthy activities such as nutritious eating and exercise.

Financial

Recovery in finances involves feeling secure with financial situations. This is often one of the most stressful areas of life for people in the early stages of recovery from alcohol and drug abuse. Developing savings, paying off credit card or other debt, and feeling confident that you can provide for yourself and your family can help achieve financial recovery.

Family

Family recovery is related to all aspects of family life. This includes feeling satisfied with your current family structure (for example, being married, not having kids), your relationships with family members, and the degree to which you feel connected to your family. It goes without saying that a person's alcohol and drug abuse affects his or her family members. In order to achieve recovery in this area, it may be necessary to discuss the affects your alcohol and drug use has had on your family and ways that you can make up for any harm you may have caused.

Social

Social recovery involves being an active member in the community and other social groups and developing healthy relationships with those around you. It also involves being comfortable expressing yourself around other people and feeling valued by others. Some people in recovery find that taking part in self-help groups enhances their social recovery.

Spiritual

Spiritual recovery happens when we are able to find peace in our lives. Spiritual recovery also involves attaining a match between our values and actions (our behaviors demonstrate what we believe in). Spirituality, as discussed here, does not have to include involvement with organized religion. Instead, it means finding meaning and believing that life is worthwhile.

Questions for Thought

1. How has your problematic substance use affected you in each of these areas?
2. How balanced is your life?

ASSESS YOUR LIFE

Use the "Wellness Wheel" on Worksheet 1 at the end of this chapter to assess your current lifestyle. For each area of life, fill in the piece of pie that corresponds to that area in terms of how well you think you fulfill that area of life. Also identify specific activities that you do within each area. You may find the example included at the end of this chapter to be helpful as you complete this worksheet.

Now, look at the final product. If your "Wellness Wheel" looks like it could "roll," you are on your way to a balanced life. If your wheel looks like it would not roll, you may have some areas to work on.

Questions for Thought

1. What is your reaction to the shape of your "Wellness Wheel"?
2. What areas do you think you need to work on? Use Worksheet 2 to identify the areas you want to improve. For each area, identify specific activities that you could do to improve.
3. How are you going to do this?

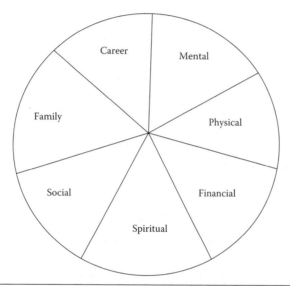

The Wellness Wheel *From Wegscheider-Cruse, S. (1989). Another chance: Hope and health for the alcoholic family. Palo Alto, CA: Science and Behavior Books.*

SUMMARY

Recovery is a lifelong endeavor and not just some endpoint you strive for. Some say you must work at your recovery on a daily basis for the rest of your life. In this chapter you learned about the concept of recovery and the stages of the recovery process. You also learned that recovery is not just about quitting alcohol and drugs; it is also about what you are going to do instead. In order to be successful in your recovery you must figure out how you are going to improve in several different areas of life. These are the life areas of career, mental, physical, financial, spiritual, social, and family. Hopefully, you found Worksheets 1 and 2 helpful to you as you plan ways to lead a complete recovery lifestyle. In the next chapter, you will learn about the process of relapse and how to prevent it from happening.

Wellness Wheel Example My Current Lifestyle

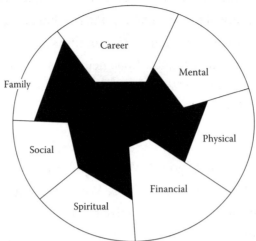

Activities I currently take part in:

Career:
I am working in a low-wage job but exploring options and other job opportunities.

_____

_____

Mental:
I generally read a book a week and spend lots of time at the library. I watch educational shows on television and am thinking of going back to
school.

_____

_____

Physical:
I work out a couple of times per week. I am trying to quit smoking. I walk my dog on a daily basis. I am thinking of taking up yoga.

_____

_____

Financial:
I have very little money and am having trouble paying my bills. Money is a constant source of stress.

_____

_____

Spiritual:
I attend church on a regular basis and am exploring other religions. I read books on philosophy and spirituality.

_____

_____

Social:
I am spending time with new friends. I am avoiding old friends that I used to use AOD with. Sometimes I get lonely and wonder
where else I can meet new people.

_____

_____

Family:
I have a very supportive family that I spend time with every week. I feel satisfied with my family interactions. I am learning new ways
to be a better parent to my children and am strengthening my relationships with my kids.

_____

_____

Worksheet 1: My Current Lifestyle

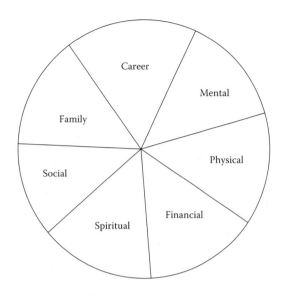

Activities I currently take part in:

Career: _____

_____

_____

Mental: _____

_____

_____

Physical: _____

_____

_____

Financial: _____

_____

_____

Spiritual: _____

_____

_____

Social: _____

_____

_____

Family: _____

_____

_____

Worksheet 2: My Recovery Lifestyle

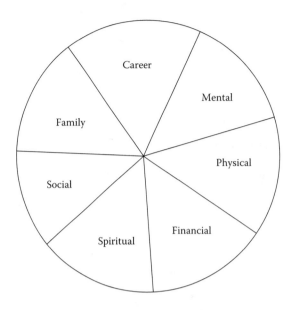

Activities I plan to take part in for my recovery:

Career: _____

_____

_____

Mental: _____

_____

_____

Physical: _____

_____

_____

Financial: _____

_____

_____

Spiritual: _____

_____

_____

Social: _____

_____

_____

Family: _____

_____

_____

NOTES

6

PREVENTING RELAPSE

In Chapter 5 you learned about the concept of recovery and what is involved in creating a healthy recovery lifestyle. One of the points made in Chapter 5 was that recovery can often involve a "slip" or "relapse." A slip or relapse involves a temporary return to problematic alcohol and drug use. In order to better understand how relapse happens and how you can prevent it, it is important to study the concept of relapse in greater detail. That is the purpose of this chapter. By the end of the chapter you should be able to:

1. Understand what relapse is and why it is occurs.
2. Understand the process of relapse.
3. Identify reasons you may have relapsed in the past.
4. Create and write down a relapse prevention plan.

WHAT IS RELAPSE?

As mentioned, relapse is defined as a return to problematic use of alcohol and drugs after entering recovery. Relapse can be an isolated incident or a return to regular use or behavioral patterns. It should be noted that relapse is often recognized as a part of the recovery process. It often takes more than one time in treatment for a person to successfully enter recovery. This does not mean, however, that a person can't be successful on his or her first attempt.

Because recovery from alcohol and drug abuse is difficult, you should not give up on recovery if you have a relapse. Instead, you should recognize it as a temporary "slip" and return to activities consistent with recovery. Recovery is difficult for a variety of reasons. Some of these reasons are listed here.

- After giving up alcohol and drugs the person in recovery is faced with numerous and intense stressors.
- The person in recovery may experience difficulty in reconnecting with family members after giving up alcohol and drugs.

- The person in recovery may find that he or she misses the excitement associated with using alcohol and drugs.
- After entering recovery it may be difficult to control emotions such as anger and sadness. The recovering substance abuser may have used alcohol and drugs as a way to cope with stress, depression, and anxiety in the past. Therefore, it may be more difficult to resist alcohol and drug use when these emotions are activated.
- The person in recovery may have a difficult time with transportation either because he or she has lost his or her driver's license or does not have a reliable way to get around.

Questions for Thought

1. Which of these reasons is most relevant to you?
2. Can you think of any other reasons that recovery may be difficult?
3. How might thinking errors contribute to the way you handle the above situations?

PATTERNS OF RELAPSE

Scientists and researchers have found a pattern to the process of relapse. They tell us that relapse begins long before a person takes his or her first drink or uses the first drug. The process is illustrated in Diagram 1 and goes as follows:

1. The person is placed in a high-risk situation. This means that he or she is in a situation that reminds him or her of alcohol and drug use. As a result the person experiences cravings and urges to use in problematic ways.
2. No coping response for this situation has been developed yet. That is, the person has not yet developed a plan to deal with the situation.
3. Because of this, the person is not confident that he or she can control the alcohol and drug use. The person may be able to handle the situation the first few times but remains unconfident. The thought of using in problematic ways is in his or her head.
4. The person then uses the alcohol and/or drugs.
5. The person feels guilty, incompetent, and as if he or she has lost control because of this initial use.
6. These feelings may then lead the person to further alcohol and drug problems.

As shown in Diagram 1, if the person had developed effective coping responses to deal with the high-risk situation, he or she would have been less likely to relapse. Also, if the person has the ability to predict and identify high-risk situations, the person will be less likely to find him- or herself in situations that lead to relapse.

Questions for Thought

1. What high-risk situations do you anticipate?
2. Do you think you have effective coping responses to deal with these situations?

RECOGNIZING YOUR RISKS

Complete Worksheets 1 and 2 to assist you in recognizing what types of risks for relapse you may encounter in your recovery. Worksheet 1 asks you to provide a summary of your relapse history. Worksheet 2 will help you to identify some warning signs or risks for relapse. Understanding why you have relapsed in the past and your risks for future relapse will help you to be more successful in your recovery.

THE RELAPSE PREVENTION PLAN

One way to help avoid relapse is to create a relapse prevention plan. The relapse prevention plan is a tool to assist people who are in recovery to deal with high-risk situations. The plan involves predicting high-risk situations and developing strategies for handling these situations. These strategies are called coping responses. You must have multiple plans and strategies to deal with multiple high-risk situations.

A metaphor may be helpful here to illustrate this concept. Establishing a plan for dealing with high-risk situations is similar to a football team establishing a game plan to win on game day. A football team has a playbook that they study and practice from during the week. They then use the plays during the game according to how the game is going, what the score is, and where they are on the field. But, the team also has backup plans. If they come to the line of scrimmage and recognize that their play will not work against the defensive play of the other team, the offensive squad can call an audible. This is a backup play that will allow them to be more effective. Without the backup plan, the team would not be effective in the situation described above.

Example: Applied to alcohol and drugs use, backup plans are helpful. Let's say John enters a high-risk situation. He has to pick up a package from his brother's house. John's brother is a heavy drinker and will probably be drunk when he gets there. He will also offer John a drink. John's first plan to handle this high-risk situation was to explain to his brother that he had quit drinking and that he would appreciate it if his brother would not offer him alcohol. John tried this and it didn't work. Therefore, he used his second plan or audible—he left the house and sent a friend back to get the package.

Questions for Thought

1. Can you think of any other effective coping behaviors for John?
2. What if it does not work, what else could he do?
3. What would you do if you were in John's situation?
4. What if it didn't work?

SUMMARY

In this chapter you learned about the process of relapse and some ways to prevent it. To finish this chapter complete Worksheet 3: The Relapse Prevention Plan. Review your answers to Worksheets

1 and 2 when completing this activity. This activity will also require you to return to worksheets you completed in previous chapters. Make sure you understand the concepts that were discussed in those chapters and why you completed the worksheets the way you did. In the next chapter we will review feelings and emotions and how they can relate to recovery and relapse prevention.

Diagram 1: The Process of Relapse

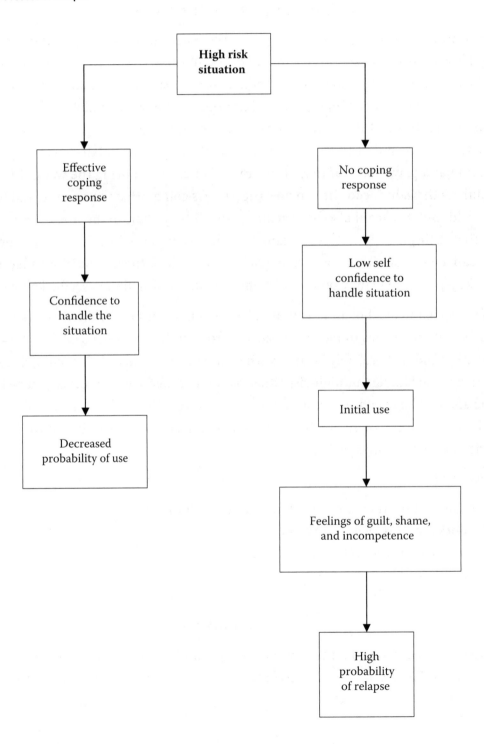

Worksheet 1: Summary of Relapse History

Purpose: In this exercise, you will work to figure out what has led you to relapse in the past.

Instructions: Answer the questions below. Remember that you do not have to fill in every line.

1. I first attempted recovery in _____ (fill in month and year).

2. Since that time, I have tried to quit using _____ times.

3. The longest I have been able to be completely free of alcohol and drugs was _____ (days, months, or years).

4. The problems that appeared more than once before I started using alcohol or drugs again are:

  A. Problems with people:

  1. _____

  2. _____

  3. _____

  4. _____

  B. Problems with situations:

  1. _____

  2. _____

  3. _____

  4. _____

  C. Problems with thoughts and feelings:

  1. _____

  2. _____

  3. _____

  4. _____

  D. Problems with pain and sickness:

  1. _____

  2. _____

  3. _____

4. These problems usually happen in the following order: _____ I started to use alcohol or drugs again when: I started to thinkI started to feel I wanted to _____. The first drug I used was (include alcohol): _____ _____Then I used:Then I used:

Source: Adapted from: U.S. Department of Health and Human Services (2004). Counselor's manual for relapse prevention with chemically dependent criminal offenders. *Treatment Assistance Publication 19. Washington, DC: SAMHSA. This instrument is in the public domain.*

Worksheet 2: Relapse Warning Signs

Purpose. This list will help you understand why you may return to using alcohol and drugs, even when you do not want to.

Instructions. Below is a list of thoughts, feelings, and actions that you may experience before relapsing. Read the list and place a checkmark next to any signs that you have experienced. Place a question mark next to any that you do not understand. Underline any words that cause you to have strong thoughts or feelings or make you want to do something. (This list was adapted from the work of Stanton E. Samenow, Ph.D.)

Phase I: Internal Dysfunction: During this period, changes occur in thoughts and feelings. These changes are unnoticed by other people.

____ 1. *Worry: I worry about being able to survive in the real world. I wonder how I am going to be able to find and keep a job, pay bills, get along with my family, or stay away from my old friends.*

____ 2. *Denial: I tell myself it will all work out. I pretend everything is all right. When people ask me about my problems, I tell them I will be okay, even though I am not sure.*

____ 3. *Belief that troubles are over: I convince myself that I've learned my lesson and will never do anything illegal again. I tell my friends, family, and counselor, "I've really learned this time," even though I do not have a plan for how to change.*

____ 4. *Uncomfortable feelings: I feel uncomfortable around people who do not use alcohol and drugs. They seem boring, and I get nervous and jumpy. I want more excitement in my life.*

____ 5. *"All or nothing" thinking: I feel like I must be the best or I will be nothing. I must be very successful at everything I do. I get excited and build up in my mind how successful I must be. I feel that if I do not do everything right, I will fail.*

____ 6. *Unrealistic feelings: I think things should go my way just because I want them to. Because other people want me to succeed and I want to do well, things will happen the way I want them to.*

____ 7. *Not planning ahead: I do not plan for the future. When people ask me what my plans are, I tell them what I think they want to hear.*

____ 8. *Lack of effort: I do not do things that I do not like or that are boring or hard for me. I do not look into jobs or other things that might help me, and I find excuses for not doing these things.*

____ 9. *Building self up: I make myself feel better by putting other people down. I tell myself how stupid other people are. Most of the time I just think it, but sometimes I tell people that they are dumb or do not know anything.*

____ 10. *Poor decision making: I make decisions on the spur of the moment without thinking about what might happen. Afterward, I think, "I really screwed up."*

____ 11. *Sensing a lack of trust: I feel like others do not agree with me or do not trust me. I think people should trust me no matter what I may have done in the past. I tell them I have changed, and I expect them to believe me. Their lack of trust makes me angry.*

Phase II: External Dysfunction: In this phase, other people start to notice that you are acting differently. Your behavior starts to cause problems with others.

____ 12. *Feeling put down: I think other people are putting me down when they point bad things out to me or when things do not happen the way I want. I think people do not understand me, and I begin to argue with them.*

____ 13. *Wanting to be alone: I start to avoid my family and other people. I wander around alone or go places by myself.*

____ 14. *Feeling depressed: I feel depressed, lonely, and angry. I don't think other people understand me. I start having problems sleeping, or I don't eat regularly and eat junk food. I feel hopeless.*

____ 15. *Denying fears: I do not want others to know I am afraid because I think being afraid is being weak. I tell people I am fine when I am really not. I'd rather tell people what they want to hear so that they won't know how I really feel.*

____ 16. *Having envious thoughts: I start to think about people I know who use alcohol and drugs it. I start to wish that I could do that, too. I wonder if there is an easier way to do things.*

Phase III: Loss of Control: Your feelings at this time seem to control you. You can't seem to get yourself back on track. You feel like you can never change and wonder why you should try.

____ 17. *Avoiding responsibility: I do what I want instead of what I told people I would do. When things go wrong, I tell people "I forgot." I either change the subject or do not give them an answer. Sometimes I say "yes" when I do not really mean it.*

____ 18. *Using alcohol or drugs: Sometimes I feel good but I want to feel better. Sometimes I feel bad and I want to escape from my feelings. I begin to use alcohol or drugs to make good feelings better or to get rid of bad feelings. At first, I keep this a secret. If my counselor or family asks me about it, I lie.*

____ 19. *Seeing old friends: I start to hang around people who use alcohol and drugs. I want to be comfortable and they are the only people who seem to understand me. I go back to my old hangouts. I call people I know who use alcohol and drugs. I tell myself I am only doing this to find out how they are doing.*

____ 20. *Missing appointments: I miss appointments with my counselor, job interviews, or school. I make up excuses as to why I wasn't there. I begin to believe these people are out to get me and I can't trust them.*

____ 21. *Thinking "I can't": I tell people I can't do something, or I don't know how when I really just do not want to. I feel afraid or angry when I think about doing things that others want me to do.*

____ 22. *Playing the victim: I blame others when things go wrong. I tell people I couldn't help it. I feel like others are picking on me or are not giving me a chance. I feel like people will never be satisfied with me.*

____ 23. *Not understanding how I hurt others: I feel like other people are always telling me that I hurt them. I do not see how the things I do may hurt other people, and sometimes I get frustrated and I do not care.*

____ 24. *Committing petty crimes: I start stealing small things. I begin using illegal drugs, destroying other people's property, or getting into fights.*

____ 25. *Rejecting others: When people ask me what is wrong, I tell them that there is nothing wrong. If they persist, I tell them to leave me alone, yell at them, or do something to make them leave me alone.*

____ 26. *Thinking that I'm always right: I don't back down when other people do not agree with me. I feel that I am never wrong no matter what. I feel if I admit to others that I am wrong, they will think I am weak and will take advantage of me. Even if it turns out I am wrong, I leave or start a fight rather than admit it.*

____ 27. *Feeling entitled to what I want: I think other people should give me what I want, when I want it. If they do not, I have a right to take it. I feel angry that they won't do what I want or give me what I want. I feel like I have to teach them a lesson.*

____ 28. *Feeling that my anger is justified: I feel that if I do not get what I want, I have the right to get angry, threaten, hurt, or get even with people. I feel I have the right to do whatever I have to because other people do not understand.*

____ 29. *Wanting to win: I feel I must win at all costs. I will do whatever it takes to get back at someone who makes me angry.*

Source: Adapted from: U.S. Department of Health and Human Services (2004). Counselor's manual for relapse prevention with chemically dependent criminal offenders. Treatment Assistance Publication 19. Washington, DC: SAMHSA. This instrument is in the public domain.

Worksheet 3: The Relapse Prevention Plan

Go back to the goals and problems that you identified on the Chapters 1, 2, and 3 worksheets. Now think about a potential high-risk situation that may lead to temptation to reengage in the behavior that you want to change. Come up with a primary plan and two backup plans for dealing with this high-risk situation. Review Worksheets 1 and 2 in this chapter to help you with this. Make copies of this sheet as you need to and identify strategies and plans for handling other potential relapse risks.

Potential High-Risk Situation:

_____

_____

_____

_____

_____

Primary Plan:

_____

_____

_____

_____

_____

Backup Plan 1:

_____

_____

_____

_____

_____

Backup Plan 2:

_____

_____

_____

_____

_____

NOTES

7

MANAGING EMOTIONS

In Chapters 5 and 6 you learned about the concepts of recovery and relapse. You also learned about some of the risks for relapse and started a relapse prevention plan. In this chapter you will learn about one major risk for relapse—having difficulty managing emotions. Then, after learning a bit about emotions, you will also learn about co-occurring disorders. The term co-occurring disorder is used to indicate that a person has a psychological disorder (e.g., depression, anxiety, etc.) in addition to a problem with alcohol or drug use.

By the end of this chapter you should be able to:

1. Identify what emotions are.
2. Understand what good emotional health is.
3. Be familiar with some tips for managing emotions.
4. Understand the symptoms of several co-occurring disorders.
5. Understand the relationship between co-occurring disorders, substance abuse problems, and relapse.

Questions for Thought

1. What does the word "emotion" mean to you?
2. How many emotions can you list on a separate piece of paper?
3. What emotions have you experienced in the past 48 hours?

WHAT ARE EMOTIONS?

Emotions are hard to define. Every definition of emotion is a bit different, but most people agree that a good definition of emotion includes the following things:

- Emotion is a mental state: emotions are experienced in our minds.
- Emotion is also a physical state: emotions are experienced in our bodies. For example, a person who is depressed often feels tired and lethargic. Likewise, a person who is angry

feels tense and has a higher heart rate. Finally, a person who is anxious may sweat and tremble.

- Emotion is a reaction to some event: we experience emotion as a reaction to something that has happened to us or to some experience we have had. For example, individuals may feel happy when they are with someone they love, angry when they are insulted by a coworker in front of the supervisor, embarrassed if they trip and fall in a public place, or jealous when they see others who have things that they don't.

- Emotion motivates us to do something: because emotions are a reaction to an event, we are motivated to do something about the event. Using the examples in the previous bullet point, the person that is happy to be with someone he or she loves may give that person a gift. The person who was embarrassed because he or she fell in a public place may turn red and quickly leave the scene. When the emotional state is negative (e.g., frustration), we are motivated to do something to get rid of that state. When it is positive, we are motivated to do what we can to experience more of it.

Early in recovery a person can expect to feel many strong emotions. Often, the person has blocked the experience of these emotions by using alcohol and drugs. Because of this, the person can expect to experience a range of reactions to these emotions. Additionally, because alcohol and drugs have been used to cope with these emotions in the past, it becomes difficult to know how to handle them. Some emotions are common to people when they enter early recovery. These emotions can possibly become overpowering and lead to relapse. These include anger, frustration, shame, jealousy, love, or fear.

At the end of this chapter you will find Figure 7.1 titled "Emotions Meter." The emotions meter demonstrates that emotions can be experienced at different levels—from mild, to moderate, to extreme. On the meter, Level 1 represents a mild emotional experience. Level 10 indicates an extreme and problematic experience of the emotion. At Level 10, the person is likely to do something he or she will regret later.

In order to live a healthy life, a person must experience all emotional states at some time. It is unrealistic to think that someone can totally quit feeling uncomfortable emotions such as anger or anxiety. It is possible, however, to learn to control emotions so that they do not rise to levels that can lead to problems.

Think about the emotions meter for a moment. Can you recall a time in the past week where you experienced an emotion at a Level 1? Level 5? Level 10? What was different about each of these instances? Make notes as needed at the end of this chapter.

Questions for Thought   How might the following emotions put you at risk for relapse?

1. Anger?
2. Frustration?
3. Stress?
4. Shame?

5. Jealousy?

6. Hate?

7. Contempt?

8. Embarrassment?

9. Anxiety?

10. Love?

WHAT IS EMOTIONAL HEALTH?

Emotional health can be defined as the successful performance of emotional functioning that allows a person to be productive, have fulfilling relationships with other people, and be able to adapt to change and adversity. Emotional health generally refers to an individual's thoughts, feelings, and actions, particularly when faced with challenges and stresses. Good emotional health isn't just the absence of emotional problems—it is an overall sense of well-being. Strong emotional health is extremely important to recovery. When a person is in good emotional health he or she often displays the following:

- An ability to enjoy life,
- Laugh often and have fun,
- An ability to deal with life's problems while continuing with their daily lives,
- Participation in personally rewarding activities,
- An ability to change as life changes,
- Experience a wide range of emotions,
- A sense of personal balance—this means not feeling overwhelmed in one area of life,
- The ability to care for self and others,
- Self-confidence and good self-esteem.

Emotional health is important for a number of reasons. These are:

- Feeling emotionally distressed can lead to physical health problems.
- Our personal relationships are directly affected by our emotional health—poor emotional health can lead to relationship problems.
- Our ability to manage daily problems is directly affected by our emotional health.
- Poor emotional health can weaken our ability to make good decisions and lead to irrational actions such as alcohol and other drug (AOD) abuse.
- Poor emotional health can lead to relapse and recidivism.

Good emotional health is extremely important to recovery from an alcohol or drug problem. Often people have used alcohol or drugs to cope with emotional problems and have not developed other, healthier ways for dealing with extreme emotional states. Gaining emotional health is therefore an important piece of recovery. By being emotionally healthy you can lessen your risk for relapse.

Questions for Thought

1. How might emotional health be incorporated into your relapse prevention plan?
2. Do you feel emotionally healthy now?
3. If not, what's missing?

THE A-B-C OF EMOTIONS

In previous chapters you learned about the A-B-C model. To review, *A* stands for the activating event, *B* for the belief or thought, and *C* for the consequent behavior or feeling. Remember that thoughts and beliefs lead to emotions and behaviors. So, this means that gaining emotional health means taking care of our problems in thinking and changing our unrealistic beliefs.

For problematic emotions, the A-B-C model would go as follows:

A	→	B	→	C
(Event)		(Irrational thought or belief)		(Level 10 emotion)

Therefore, in order to experience emotions at healthy levels—and to avoid reaching a 9 or 10 on the emotions meter—you will need to change any irrational beliefs or thoughts you may have about the world and things that happen to you.

Think about the following example and the questions for thought that follow. Try to apply the concepts from the A-B-C and strategic thinking models as well as the emotions meter as you consider the example.

Example: John was driving to work at 7:30 in the morning. He has never been a morning person and it was hard for him to get up, especially since he only got 3 hours of sleep. He was pulling off his street when another car sped in front of him, almost causing an accident. John became so angry that he cursed as loud as he could and punched the windshield of his car. The windshield broke and there was glass all over his car. John also broke his hand and had to go to the hospital. He missed work that day. When he went back he got fired for missing work. After all, said his supervisor, he was new and the company had done him a favor in hiring him—nobody else in town would hire someone without much experience.

Questions for Thought

1. What was the activating event?
2. What irrational thoughts do you think John was having?
3. What emotions do you think John was experiencing?
4. What level do you think those emotions were at?
5. What could John have done differently so that he did not reach such a high level on the emotions meter?
6. How could he have thought differently about the situation?

7. Now, replace the irrational thought with a rational one—how would you rewrite this story?

Sometime during the next week use Worksheet 1 to examine the A-B-Cs of a situation you experience that raised a strong emotion(s) for you.

TIPS FOR MANAGING EMOTIONS

In addition to analyzing problematic thoughts and beliefs, several basic self-care and lifestyle issues can also help increase emotional health. This information builds off of the concept of wellness in recovery presented in Chapter 5. Some of these are listed below.

1. Getting enough rest.
2. Eating a diet that includes fruit, vegetables, and required daily vitamins.
3. Avoid eating fast food on a regular basis.
4. Reduce caffeine and nicotine intake—these are "uppers" that can lead to agitation.
5. Exercise on a regular basis.
6. Take time to do relaxing things that you enjoy on a regular basis.
7. Prioritize things that you need to take care of—do the most important first.
8. Associate with positive people.
9. Know the effects of your medications—some can lead to increased agitation.

Some things to avoid include:

1. Alcohol and drugs.
2. Chaotic living situations—this will make it harder to relax.
3. Isolation from friends and family.
4. Excessive conflict with others, especially those who have power over you (e.g., supervisors).
5. Ignoring or not dealing with painful events (death of a loved one, loss of a job, etc.).

To achieve good emotional health means that you have to manage stress, frustrations, anxiety, and anger on a daily basis—*not just when it becomes a problem!* When stress and anxiety build up over time, we become less able to deal with everyday problems.

For example, people will react differently to common daily problems such as being cut off while driving. In the example of John above:

- The emotionally unhealthy person may become enraged at being cut off. They are carrying around so much other stress that this one event pushes them over the edge.
- The emotionally healthy person has already managed his or her daily stress. Therefore, that person is able to cope with his or her feelings of anger at being cut off by another driver— the person doesn't have a lot of other stresses weighing on his or her mind.

Finally, in order to become emotionally healthy a person must create a plan to deal with emotions when they arise. This is similar to the relapse prevention plan you have already started to create.

PSYCHOLOGICAL PROBLEMS RELATED TO AOD ABUSE

In some cases strong emotional states can turn into more severe forms of emotional problems. These are often called psychological disorders and can be strongly related to AOD abuse. That is to say, people who have an AOD problem are more likely to have some form of a psychological disorder. There has been a stigma attached to the term psychological disorder; some people think of it as being "crazy," "insane," or "disturbed." It is important for you to understand that there is no shame in having a psychological disorder. It is also important that you get help for it.

Psychological Disorder

The term "psychological" refers to those things that are related to our thoughts, emotions, feelings, and ability to cope with our environment. Psychological disorders are sometimes defined as occurring when a person's mental functioning is unusual or significantly different from "normal." When a psychological disorder exists, the person may be experiencing some distress, including unpleasant or upsetting thoughts or feelings. Psychological disorders make it hard for a person to manage daily activities. Finally, in extreme cases, the person may become a danger to him- or herself (for example, suicide) or others.

Some examples of psychological disorders are:

- Extreme depression,
- Unmanageable anxiety,
- Traumatic stress,
- Bipolar disorder (manic-depression),
- Attention deficit hyperactivity disorder (ADHD).

Co-Occurring Disorder

Co-occurring disorders used to be called comorbid disorders or dual diagnosis disorders. In case you ever hear these terms, you will have an idea about what they mean. A co-occurring disorder exists when a person has both a psychological disorder and an alcohol and drug problem. Sometimes, psychological disorders can lead a person to use alcohol and drugs. For example, a depressed person may use alcohol to forget his or her problems. Alcohol and drug abuse can also lead to psychological problems. Some researchers believe, for example, that use of Ecstasy can lead to long-term depression.

When a person uses alcohol or drugs to lessen symptoms such as stress, anxiety, anger, hyperactivity, or depression they are said to be *self-medicating*. This means that they are using AOD to sooth symptoms of a psychological disorder.

Example: Julie started drinking alcohol and using marijuana when she was 16 years old. It was around that time that her mother died from cancer. After her mother died, Julie's father spent more time at work and was generally withdrawn from the rest of the family. Julie began to feel lonely and depressed. She found that when she drank or used drugs she felt less lonely and was able to relax and have a good time.

Several psychological disorders are common to people with alcohol and drug problems. Some symptoms of these are presented on the sheet titled "Common Psychological Problems" at the end of this chapter.

Questions for Thought

1. Have you experienced any of the symptoms from the "Common Psychological Problems" sheet at the end of the chapter?
2. Have you noticed that when you use AOD these symptoms are less intense?
3. Did you experience the symptoms prior to the time when you began using AOD for the first time?

Worksheet 2 can help you answer these questions.

What to Do If You Experience Any of These Symptoms

Several options for getting help for a co-occurring disorder are listed below. If you are experiencing any of the symptoms described in this chapter during your recovery it is important that you get help immediately. If you don't, you are increasing your risk for alcohol and drug relapse. Below are some suggested ways to get help for a co-occurring disorder. When approaching these or other sources, be sure to explain that you might have symptoms of a psychological disorder *and* that you have a history of alcohol and drug abuse or dependence. The fact that you are experiencing both will impact the type of treatment that is offered to you. You need to be open and honest to make sure you get the best help.

- *Get a professional opinion.* Get an assessment to see whether or not what you are experiencing is a psychological disorder or just part of normal, everyday emotional life.
- *Get substance abuse treatment.* If you have a history of alcohol and drug abuse, get help.
- *Tell your substance abuse counselor.* This is especially important. If you are in treatment, let someone know about your symptoms. If you don't, you may not be receiving the most effective treatment.
- *Tell a friend or family member.* Sometimes just telling another person will increase your motivation to do something about your symptoms.
- *Tell your doctor.* Your doctor may know about treatment options or be able to provide treatment him- or herself. Make sure your doctor also knows you have a history of AOD abuse.
- *Locate your community mental health center and contact them.* Inexpensive treatment options may be available to you.
- *Most importantly, be assertive and get help.* There is no shame in experiencing these symptoms and effective treatments are out there to help you. There is no need to continue to suffer. You will also be more stable in your recovery if you address these issues.

SUMMARY

Having worked through this chapter you should now understand what emotions are and have some ideas on how to handle them when they come up. You should also be familiar with the term co-occurring disorder and understand the importance of paying attention to any psychological symptoms you may be experiencing. If you do have any of the psychological symptoms presented in this chapter, get help from a licensed professional. *It is important to remember that if you do not get help for a co-occurring psychological problem you are at a higher risk for relapse.* In the next chapter you will learn how to create a new lifestyle that is free from AOD abuse.

The Emotions Meter

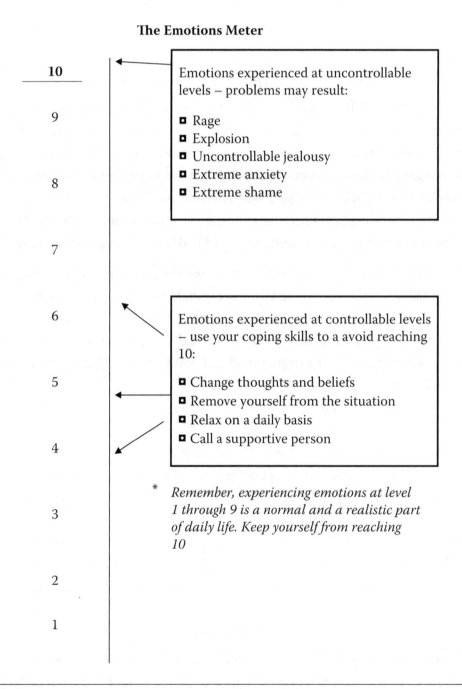

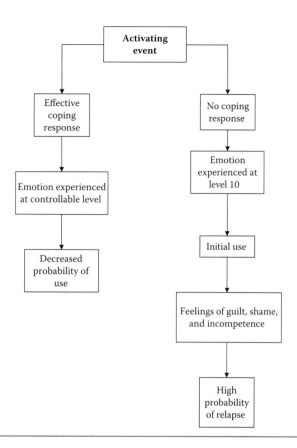

Activating Event

Common Psychological Problems

Depression	Serious depression is more than just having a low mood or feeling the "blues." For serious depression to be diagnosed as a psychological disorder, the person must experience: (a) extreme sadness or feelings of being down for at least 2 weeks straight, (b) feelings of hopelessness, (c) negative views of self, others, and the future (e.g., "I'll never amount to anything"), (d) problems concentrating, (e) withdrawal from others, (f) increased or decreased sleep, (g) thoughts of death or self-harm, (h) extreme feelings of guilt, and (i) low motivation to do anything.
Bipolar disorder	Bipolar disorder used to be called manic-depression. This psychological disorder leads to extreme mood swings that are different from normal, everyday changes in mood. These mood swings range from strong feelings of exhilaration and self-confidence to symptoms of depression described above. When the person is "up" they experience extreme self-confidence, irrational thinking, racing thoughts, and low desire for sleep or food. When the person is "down" they experience the symptoms of depression.
Anxiety disorder	Anxiety disorders are different from experiencing everyday anxiety; say mild anxiety related to public speaking. This type of anxiety involves extreme worry, strong tension or fear, difficulty in concentrating, avoidance or withdrawal of others, avoidance of situations that are associated with anxiety, and obsessing on the anxious feelings.
Traumatic stress	Traumatic stress results from experiencing a traumatic event at some point in life. This may be physical, sexual, or emotional abuse, or experiencing or seeing a life-threatening event. People with traumatic stress often relive the experience through nightmares and flashbacks, have difficulty sleeping, and feel "different" from everyone else. These symptoms can be severe enough and last long enough to significantly impair the person's daily life.
Attention deficit hyperactivity disorder (ADHD)	ADHD is a problem often seen in children, but adults can also have the symptoms of it. ADHD is a problem that is just like it sounds. A person with ADHD has problems keeping their attention on something. They may also be constantly unable to sit still, concentrate, or finish projects that they have started. These symptoms may lead to problems in school or work.

Source: Information adapted from Evans, K., & Sullivan, J. (2001). Dual diagnosis: Counseling the mentally ill substance abuser (2nd ed.). New York: Guilford.

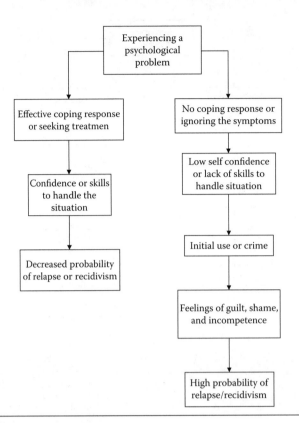

Cooccurring Disorders and Relapse

Worksheet 1: Emotions Log

Complete this sheet for an experience with an emotion that you have this week.

What was the emotion?

_____

_____

_____

What was the emotions meter level?

_____

_____

_____

What was the activating event?

_____

_____

_____

What were your thoughts about the event?

_____

_____

_____

How did you respond?

_____

_____

_____

What could you have done differently?

_____

_____

_____

Worksheet 2: Recognizing the Symptoms

Use the spaces below to answer the questions in each column. Your responses to column 3 will remain confidential.

Psychological Disorder	What Symptoms Could Lead to Relapse/Recidivism?	What Symptoms, If Any, Have I Experienced?

Depression

Bipolar disorder

Anxiety disorder

Traumatic stress

Attention deficit hyperactivity disorder (ADHD)

NOTES

8

LIVING WITH INTEGRITY

Hopefully, if you have made it this far in this book, you have taken a long, hard look at yourself, your motivation to change, your thinking patterns, and your emotions as they relate to alcohol and other drug (AOD) abuse and recovery. In this chapter, you will begin the tasks necessary to maintain all of the changes you have created thus far. Learning to live and communicate with integrity is essential in these endeavors.

It has been said that addiction takes place in the dark, while recovery takes place in the light. While engaging in harmful AOD use, you may have found that you lived by a certain set of anti-social values. You may have tried to hide your AOD use from others, manipulated family and friends to buy AOD, lied to others about your activities and behaviors, and generally lived a secretive lifestyle. However, now that you are working toward recovery, living in the dark and hiding your true thoughts, feelings, and emotions from others is no longer an option. To be successful in recovery you must be honest with yourself and others about all aspects of your life. This is the foundation to living life with integrity.

This chapter is designed to help you change your lifestyle once and for all. After working through this chapter you should:

1. Understand the concept of integrity and why it is important to recovery.
2. Understand the basic styles of communication and learn to communicate effectively with others.
3. Understand the way that interactions between people occur.
4. Develop a list of alternative activities to AOD use.
5. Create a plan for maintaining the changes you have made.

DEFINING INTEGRITY

Integrity involves being true to yourself, having your own ideas and not being afraid to share them, not agreeing with others just to be accepted, and generally living by your own pro-social values and beliefs. Living with integrity involves:

1. Keeping your word.

2. Being reliable.

3. Doing what you say you are going to do.

4. Treating others with respect.

5. Treating yourself with respect.

6. Following all laws and rules of society, regardless of whether you agree with them or not.

7. Living drug and alcohol free.

8. Living crime free.

9. Making your voice heard.

10. Making your needs known to others.

11. Compromising.

12. Accepting that you may not always get your way.

13. Speaking the truth, even if it may cause tension or conflict.

14. Admitting to yourself and others when you have done something wrong, acted inappropriately, or made a mistake.

15. Admitting to yourself and others that you don't have all of the answers—not misrepresenting yourself as an expert in some area that you have no experience.

Questions for Thought

1. Why is it important to live with integrity during your recovery?

2. What might happen if you are dishonest in your recovery?

3. Can you think of any instances where you have not lived with integrity in recent months? What was the outcome?

BECOMING A PERSON OF INTEGRITY

In previous chapters pro-social and anti-social values were discussed. Pro-social values are those values that show respect for others and self, contribute to the good of society—or at least do not harm others—and demonstrate a commitment to follow rules and laws of society. Anti-social values, on the other hand, are those values that show a disregard for the rights of others, rules and laws, and a disrespect of society in general.

Having or knowing pro-social values does not automatically mean that someone will live by those values. For example, many people know that smoking is not healthy. Smoking can cause personal illness and illness to those around them through secondhand smoke. However, even though we know that smoking is bad, many of us still do it. Likewise, everyone knows that speeding is against the law and speed limit signs are posted everywhere. Despite this, most people drive over the speed limit on a regular basis. So, it is not enough to have pro-social values, we must live by those values to be successful in recovery. Having pro-social values *and* living by those values is what integrity is all about.

Use Worksheet 1 at the end of this chapter to explore your values. Using this worksheet you will identify values that are important to you and determine ways that you will live according to those values.

COMMUNICATING WITH INTEGRITY

Having strong communication skills is a key ingredient to living with integrity and having success in recovery. In recovery, good communication is crucial to getting along with others, asking for help, and telling others about our needs. It is also an essential component of being able to talk about those things that are hard for us to do in our recovery. Several important aspects of communication are described in this section.

Communication Basics

Good communication is the foundation for getting things done in life (Johnson, 2003). It is also required to build constructive and positive relationships, which is of major importance in a person's recovery from problematic AOD use. When a person has good communication skills it means that he or she is effective in interpersonal situations (i.e., interactions between two or more people). There are several basic characteristics of interpersonal effectiveness. Good communication skills and interpersonal effectiveness are characterized by:

1. *Mutual respect:* respecting others and respecting yourself during interpersonal interactions.

2. *Trust:* placing trust in others and being trustworthy with what has been shared with you.

3. *Honesty:* this characteristic does not need an explanation! Tell the truth, no matter how painful.

4. *Appropriate self-disclosure:* letting others know something about you, letting others get to know you. However, self-disclosure must be appropriate to the situation. An example of appropriate self-disclosure may involve sharing feelings about recovery in a support group. An example of inappropriate self-disclosure, on the other hand, would be sharing your history of abuse with a stranger next to you on the bus. Inappropriate self-disclosure can serve to push people away and alienate you from others.

5. *Expressing feelings appropriately:* this includes managing emotions such as anger and frustration so that they do not destroy or hurt your relationships.

6. *Being true to yourself:* having your own ideas and not being afraid to share them; not agreeing with others just to be accepted.

7. *Listening to others:* good communication and interpersonal effectiveness is not just about communicating a message to others; it is also about listening to others and being interested in what they have to say. In other words, listen to others as you want them to listen to you—you might just learn something!

8. *Facing internal barriers to communication:* sometimes in recovery people want to retreat inward and avoid communicating with others. This characteristic involves facing and overcoming anxiety and stress about communicating.

9. *A match between verbal and nonverbal communication:* we communicate both with our words and our body language. Body language includes things such as posture, facial expressions, and eye contact. These should match up with what you are saying during interpersonal interactions. Crying while saying everything is great or yawning when telling someone else you are interested in what they are saying are poor examples of this skill.

To find out more about your communication skills complete Worksheet 2 at the end of this chapter.

Questions for Thought

1. Before you completed Worksheet 2, how would you have rated yourself as a communicator?
2. What did you learn about yourself after completing the exercise?
3. Why might good communication be important to recovery from an AOD abuse problem?

Communication Styles and Communicating Needs

As described above communicating needs is an important part of interpersonal effectiveness and integrity. It is generally thought that there are three ways to communicate needs: passively, aggressively, and assertively.

Passive communication really isn't communication at all. This style of communication involves having needs but not telling others what they are. It involves ignoring your own needs and giving in to the wishes of others.

> *Example:* Bill wants to talk with his girlfriend about keeping alcohol in the house. Bill is in recovery from an alcohol problem and believes that having it in his home will put him at risk for relapse. His girlfriend likes to have an occasional drink and says that she wants to be able to have it around. Instead of talking to her about this subject, Bill just accepts what she says and does not communicate his feelings.

Questions for Thought

1. What was wrong with this response?
2. What do you think might happen to Bill?

In the above example Bill does not have his needs taken into account. It is important to note that even if he had made his needs known, he might not have gotten his way. However, he would have at least been true to himself and honest with his girlfriend.

Passive communication goes against many of the characteristics of interpersonal effectiveness. It can lead to resentment of others. Not taking care of ourselves means that others are trampling on our needs.

Aggressive communication also goes against many of the characteristics of interpersonal effectiveness. The aggressive person communicates needs but does so in a disrespectful and negative way. The aggressive communicator does not take the needs of others into account, but rather insists that his needs come first, no matter what. Aggressive communication is about being selfish.

> *Example:* Bill does not want alcohol in the house. His girlfriend disagrees with him. She says she just wants to keep a small amount in the house. Bill explodes at this and begins yelling and screaming. He gets in his girlfriends face and tells her it is either his way or she can leave. Bill leaves the situation angry and his girlfriend leaves hurt.

Questions for Thought

1. What was wrong with this response?
2. What do you think might happen to Bill and his girlfriend in this situation?

Although Bill may have been correct in his need to keep alcohol out of the house for the sake of his recovery, his approach did not help the situation. He did not communicate the reason for his needs and ended up making the situation worse. Now, neither party is happy with the outcome, and Bill and his girlfriend do not understand each other's point of view.

Assertive communication is the most effective method of communication. It holds all of the characteristics of interpersonal effectiveness. Assertiveness is about acknowledging all opinions as important. Assertive communication involves the following:

- Being clear about what you feel, what you need, and how it can be achieved.
- Being able to communicate calmly without attacking another person.
- Saying "yes" when you want to, and saying "no" when you mean "no" (rather than agreeing to do something just to please someone else).
- Deciding on, and sticking to, clear boundaries—being happy to defend your position, even if it provokes conflict.
- Being confident about handling conflict if it occurs.
- Understanding how to negotiate if two people want different outcomes.
- Being able to talk openly about yourself and being able to listen to others.
- Having confident, open body language.
- Being able to give and receive positive and negative feedback.
- Having a positive, optimistic outlook.

Assertive communication involves respecting others, taking risks, not expecting to get your way, being honest about your needs, listening to others, and cooperating to resolve any problems.

Questions for Thought

1. Using the example of Bill, how could he communicate his needs in an assertive way?
2. What is his body language likely to look like?
3. What do you think the outcome will be?

UNDERSTANDING INTERACTIONS

Having now discussed the characteristics of interpersonal effectiveness and the different communication styles, it will be helpful to understand the basics of interpersonal interactions. These concepts are a little more advanced so you may want to take extra time and review the material in this section more than once.

Linear Causality

Part of interpersonal effectiveness and integrity is realizing that you cannot control other people and other people cannot control you. Often we believe that someone else causes our reactions, actions, and feelings during a situation. For example, Bob says, "I got angry because the boss accused me of lying. I had no choice but to yell at him." Bob's boss fired him on the spot. This type of thinking is called *linear causality* and is shown in the diagram below:

Person
A
→
Person
B

We can use this diagram to understand Bob's situation. In this diagram, Person A is Bob's boss and Person B is Bob. According to Bob, his boss came to him and accused him of lying. Bob says that this *caused* him to react in an angry way. If this is true, Bob's boss has control over his feelings and reactions, and Bob has no control over his own behavior.

Questions for Thought

1. Do you think Bob is right?
2. What style of communication was Bob using (passive, aggressive, assertive)?
3. Can you identify any thinking errors in this situation?
4. How might Bob have handled this situation differently?
5. What would the outcome have been?

Circular Causality

In reality, others do not have control over our reactions and emotions, only we do. This is the basis for cognitive-behavioral therapy discussed in previous units. Although we cannot control the actions of others, we can influence the way a situation will be resolved. In other words, the way I treat someone may influence the way he or she treats me. This is called *circular causality* and is diagramed below.

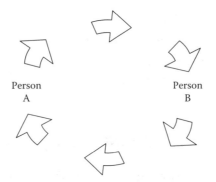

As shown in this diagram, Person B's behavior is influenced by Person A's behavior. Then, Person B's response influences Person A's behavior. For example, suppose Bob's boss accused him of lying and Bob responded calmly by asking his boss to describe what was happening.

Questions for Thought

1. What might the boss's reaction have been then?
2. Is it possible that the outcome of the situation may have been different?
3. How do you think the boss would react if Bob reacted passively? Assertively?
4. Play the tape forward on this interaction. What is likely to happen?

The main point here is that the way we respond to others affects the way they respond to us. Use Worksheet 3 to explore a recent interaction you had with someone.

NEW WAYS TO ENJOY LIFE

Aside from communication, another major aspect of living with integrity involves changing your lifestyle to match your new ways of thinking and interacting with others. In this section you will begin to think about new and healthy behaviors to take part in once you have entered recovery. You began thinking about these activities in previous chapters. If you need to, go back and review your responses to the activities in those chapters.

If you think about all of the time you spent looking for and using alcohol and drugs you may notice that these activities took up a good portion of your time. Once in recovery, the question becomes "What are you going to do with all of this free time once you quit using AOD?" Quitting alcohol and drug use is only the first step in solving your problems. You also have to consider what you are going to do instead of using AOD.

The first step toward creating new ways to enjoy life is to reflect on previous behaviors. Consider the amount of time you used to spend in problem behaviors such as AOD use. Use Worksheet 4 to help you with this.

Questions for Thought

1. What are your reactions to this exercise?
2. Were you surprised by your responses?
3. What do you think would happen if you simply removed your problem behaviors and activities and did not replace them with something else?

Generating Alternatives to Use

Now that you understand how you used to spend your days before entering recovery, it is time to generate alternatives to AOD use. It is important to point out that alternatives must be *realistic*. For example, if you do not have much money, it is not realistic for you to take up an expensive hobby such as golf.

The first step to generating ideas for alternatives to AOD use is to brainstorm. *Brainstorming* is an activity that involves coming up with several possibilities for solving a problem. When brainstorming you should:

1. Say whatever comes to mind, no matter how weird or crazy it sounds.
2. Hold off evaluating possible alternatives while generating the list.
3. Evaluate the list when completed to determine how realistic each item is.

Some ideas you can add to your list of possibilities are presented below. However, don't stop there. Come up with your own ideas. The ideas below are some things that others have found helpful in their recovery. These may or may not be helpful for you, and you should try to come up with other types of activities to include in your new lifestyle.

- Exercise
- Art
- Sports
- Volunteering
- Taking up an instrument
- Creating and maintaining close social relationships
- Reading
- Returning to school

Questions for Thought

1. What activity on your list are you most interested in?
2. Is it realistic for you?
3. What items are you least interested in? Why?
4. Are the activities that you chose going to fulfill any needs or goals that you will have in your life once you quit alcohol and drug use and criminal behavior?

Once you have identified several possible activities you should begin to consider possible roadblocks or obstacles to engaging in these activities. For example:

- Someone may identify hunting as a possible activity. If that person has a felony, however, he or she may be unable to get a gun permit.
- Someone who wants to take up basketball, but has severe arthritis in his or her knees, may have some difficulty with the new activity.
- Traveling might not be a good option for those without a good form of transportation.
- Someone may want to take up a musical instrument but have limited financial funds to buy an instrument and take lessons.

For each alternative activity on your list identify any possible obstacles to engaging in that activity.

Encountering roadblocks does not mean that you have to give up on an activity. Instead, you can *problem solve* to find ways to modify the activity to fit realistically into your life. You may, however, encounter some activities that will simply not be possible for you to take part in. If this happens, consider the following questions:

1. What appeals to you about the activity?
2. What needs do you think that activity could meet?
3. How could you have those needs met another way? In other words, are there certain activities that you can engage in that will meet your needs in a different way?

Use Worksheet 5 to complete your exploration of new alternatives to AOD use. This worksheet will guide you through the process of generating possible alternatives, evaluating how realistic those alternatives are, identifying any roadblocks to engaging in the activity, and solving any problems related to those roadblocks. Worksheet 5 will also help you to think about how you will get started with these new activities. You should review your responses to worksheets in previous chapters to help you complete Worksheet 5.

SUMMARY

There are many aspects to living with integrity, all of which are important to your recovery. In this chapter you explored your values and learned about ways to live in accordance with those values, examined your style of communication and improved your interpersonal skills, and developed new ways to enjoy life while in recovery. Each of these concepts and skill sets will be extremely important to you as you maintain all of the positive changes you have made while working through this book.

Worksheet 1: Values

Living with integrity can be a difficult thing to do. It is not always easy to stand by your word and beliefs, and to live by your own pro-social values and morals. This can be especially difficult in recovery. People in recovery often have a history of dishonesty, manipulation of others, and a general lack of respect for self and others. This exercise is designed to help you make changes to the way you live your life and interact with others. Identify the three values that are most important to you. List each in the space below and answer the questions.

Value 1:	Value 2:	Value 3:

Why is this value important to me?

_____

_____

_____

_____

How have I ignored this value or hurt others in the past?

_____

_____

_____

_____

How will I use this value to help me in recovery from alcohol, drugs, and criminal behavior?

_____

_____

_____

_____

How hard will this be for me? Explain.

_____

_____

_____

_____

Source: Information adapted from Hazelden, (2002). Socialization: A cognitive behavioral treatment curriculum. *Center City, MN: Hazelden Press.*

Worksheet 2: Communication Self-Assessment

Answer the following questions. Use the scale below to score yourself on each item:

| *Always true for me* | 5 | 4 | 3 | 2 | 1 | *Never true for me* |

Be sure to answer honestly, even if it is hard to do. Being honest with yourself is the first step to a healthy recovery.

_____ *I disclose information about myself in ways that match the situation I am in.*

_____ *When communicating, I own my ideas and am honest about what I believe in.*

_____ *I describe how I am feeling with others during conversations.*

_____ *I tell the truth rather than what people want to hear.*

_____ *I recognize and manage my anger and frustration when dealing with others.*

_____ *I make sure that my verbal and nonverbal behaviors match up.*

_____ *I listen when others are speaking and try to understand what they are saying.*

_____ *I take risks when talking with others; I share things that make me anxious or stressed out.*

_____ *I respond to others in an honest way when they ask for my opinion.*

_____ *I respect other's viewpoints, even if I do not agree with them.*

Source: Adapted from: Johnson, D. (2003). Reaching out: Interpersonal effectiveness and self-actualization. (8th ed.). New York: Allyn and Bacon: Worldwide

Worksheet 3: Personal Reflection

Take a moment to reflect on an interaction you recently had with someone where you needed to communicate your needs.

Describe the interaction: _____

_____

_____

_____

How did you respond? _____

_____

_____

_____

What communication style did you use (passive, aggressive, assertive)? _____

_____

_____

_____

What was the other person's response? _____

_____

_____

_____

What was the outcome? Did you feel successful? _____

_____

_____

_____

How might the other person's response have changed if you had communicated differently? _____

_____

_____

_____

Worksheet 4: Activity and Behavioral History

Think back to how you used to spend your days and weeks before you made the decision to quit using alcohol and drugs. Fill in the following worksheet to report how you spent a typical day.

Time	What I Typically Did
8 a.m.	
9 a.m.	
10 a.m.	
11 a.m.	
12 noon	
1 p.m.	
2 p.m.	
3 p.m.	
4 p.m.	
5 p.m.	
6 p.m.	
7 p.m.	
8 p.m.	
9 p.m.	
10 p.m.	
11 p.m.	
12 a.m.	
1 a.m.	
2 a.m.–8 a.m.	

Worksheet 5: Personal Alternatives

After finishing Worksheet 4 use the worksheet below to identify activities you may want to engage in when in recovery. Answer the questions in each column. Keep this worksheet in a visible place after you have completed it to remind you what you will do each day to avoid problematic alcohol and drug use.

Activity	Obstacles or Roadblocks	Solution for Dealing With the Obstacle	What Can I Do Today to Start Engaging in This Activity?

Source: Adapted from Velasquez, M., Maurer, G., Crouch, C., & DiClemente, C. (2001). Group treatment for substance abuse: A stages-of-change therapy manual. New York: Guilford.

NOTES

9

SUMMING UP AND MOVING FORWARD

Congratulations are certainly in order as you begin this chapter! If you have made it to this point you have worked hard, completed many difficult assignments and worksheets, and thought a great deal about changing your life. Change is difficult and it is often easier to give up rather than confront the difficulties in doing something different. So, again, I commend you.

In Chapter 1 the principles of effective learning were presented. If you remember, researchers tell us that adults learn best when they (a) hear or read new information, (b) gain an understanding of why the material is relevant to their lives, (c) practice new skills related to the information, and (d) reflect on the previous three tasks (Kolb, 1981). Another important task in effective learning is reviewing the new information you have learned and taking another look at what you have done with that information. Therefore, this chapter is designed to help you review what you have studied thus far in the book and maintain the changes you have created.

REVIEW

In the preceding chapters you read a lot of information, thought a lot about your life, set several goals, identified many strategies for change, and genuinely worked hard to make changes. Take a moment to catch your breath! As you think back on all you learned you may feel a bit overwhelmed. So, a brief summary of each chapter may be in order to help you organize your thoughts and feelings about all the work you have done. Each chapter is summarized below.

- In the first chapter of this book you identified some things you wanted to change, your reasons for wanting to change them, the positives and negatives of change, and your degree of confidence that you can make change happen.
- Next, in Chapter 2 you learned about the change process, clarified your values related to change, identified specific behaviors you wanted to change, and assessed your readiness to change.
- Cognitive-behavior theory and strategic thinking were presented in Chapter 3. As exercises in Chapter 3 you pinpointed several dysfunctional thoughts that may have

influenced your previous substance abuse, and learned a bit more about how the thinking process works.

- Then, in Chapter 4, you identified several errors in thinking that you may have used in the past and discovered how you might replace those thinking errors with functional thoughts.
- Chapter 5 was all about recovery. You learned about the recovery process and set goals for yourself on how to live a more balanced life. The "Wellness Wheel" was the main tool used to help you do this.
- Following this, in Chapter 6, you read about the process of relapse. To better understand relapse you summarized your relapse history, identified several relapse warning signs, and set an initial relapse prevention plan.
- Having difficulty managing emotions and co-occurring disorders can be one major risk for relapse. Chapter 7 provided information on this topic, gave skills for managing emotions, and helped you assess whether or not you might have a co-occurring psychological disorder. Again, remember there is no shame in having symptoms of a co-occurring disorder, so get help if you have any of the symptoms presented in Chapter 7.
- Finally, in Chapter 8 you were introduced to the concepts of integrity and communication. You also outlined a plan for how to live your life without alcohol and drugs.

That's a lot! If you are feeling overloaded by all of this, take a little time off before moving ahead with this chapter. Let the material sink in and come back in a day or two. There is no use rushing into this final chapter if you are not comfortable with all the material you have reviewed this far.

Questions for Thought

1. As you review all of this information, what are your thoughts and feelings?
2. Do you think that you worked as hard as you could at each of the activities in this book? Why or why not?
3. What chapters and activities could you have put more effort into? If any, go back and try them again.

PUTTING IT ALL TOGETHER AND LOOKING AHEAD

Now that you are at this point of the book, take a moment to examine your current situation and identify the characteristics of the "keeping it permanent" stage of change that fit with what you are doing now. Remember, characteristics of this stage, also called the maintenance stage, include (a) a commitment to a new lifestyle, (b) a strong resolve to stick to your change plan, and (c) consistent participation in new and interesting activities. If you do not think you are firmly in the maintenance stage of change, think about what life would look like if you were there. Use Worksheet 1 to help you with this.

Now, let's write the story of your future. Imagining what your life will look like in the future after you have maintained your changes can be a powerful and motivating factor to keep your changes permanent. Worksheet 2 can help you with this task. This worksheet asks you to imagine what your life will look like 5 years from now. When completing this worksheet, you will specifically identify how you have maintained the changes you laid out in each of the previous eight chapters and what your life will look like because of these changes. The worksheet asks you to visualize how your life is going to be different when you have been successful in meeting your goals. This may take a while so put it down and come back to it as many times as you need to.

After you are done, put Worksheet 2 in a place where you can see it on a regular basis. This worksheet is the story of your future, and reviewing it often will help keep you focused on what you are working toward. Of course, as we change, our goals can be altered and modified. So, as your goals for change become different, redo Worksheet 2 to reflect these differences.

MOVING FORWARD AND GETTING HELP

As you begin this section of the chapter you should be aware that the major portion of your work in this book is done! This does not mean, however, that it is time to put your goals for change away. Instead, it means that through all of your hard work you have laid the foundation for your future. The remainder of this chapter provides information on what to do next if you need further help. Even if you feel relatively comfortable and confident with the changes you have made and do not believe that you need any further assistance at this time, review the information below for future reference. You may need some help at some time, and knowing where you can get it can be a crucial first step in maintaining your change.

Now that you have finished the major portion of work in this book you may be interested to know more about the numerous types of treatment available to you. Treatment can come in many different forms and modalities. These are discussed below.

Before getting involved in treatment you can expect to take part in a comprehensive alcohol and other drug (AOD) and mental health assessment. During the assessment process, you will be asked numerous personal questions about AOD use, family history and relationships, criminal history, physical and mental health, past treatment experiences, and goals for treatment. The results of this assessment will determine the type of treatment you will take part in.

FORMATS OF TREATMENT

After the assessment, you may be referred for treatment. Once in treatment you will create a plan that specifies goals or expected outcomes for treatment (similar to the relapse prevention plan you have already worked on). Several formats of treatment are available to you and may be included in your treatment plan. These include the following.

Individual Counseling

In individual counseling the client meets one-on-one with a counselor. The client and counselor discuss AOD use, psychological or emotional issues, relapse and recidivism prevention, and problem-solving strategies to increase success in recovery.

Couple and Family Counseling

In couple or family counseling the client and selected partners or family members meet with a counselor. Issues addressed include those that are addressed in individual counseling. But the counselor and couple/family also talk about communication, child rearing, reconnecting with each other, and other relationship issues.

Group Counseling

Most clients will be referred for group counseling as this is the most widely used type of treatment in the AOD field. In group counseling the client meets with a counselor and several other clients who have the same types of issues as the client. The group may be topic focused or open discussion. The counselor may teach on certain topics or encourage group members to discuss personal issues. What is said in group counseling remains in group counseling—strict confidentiality is enforced. Persons who break confidentiality are usually removed from the group.

MODALITIES OF TREATMENT

In addition to these formats, treatment is also offered in several different settings. These are called modalities of treatment. The modalities of treatment available to you are presented in the following table.

Modality	Desired Outcome
Detoxification and short-term residential	May last 3 to 7 days depending on AOD of abuse
	Become physically stabilized from withdrawal
	Become ready for treatment
	Your motivation for treatment will increase
	You will receive a referral for ongoing treatment
Residential	May last 30–90 days
	Gain knowledge of addiction processIdentify personal problems including history of trauma, anger management, errors in thinking
	Identify strengthsEngage in cognitive restructuring—personal insight, acceptance of problematic behaviors, increased self-esteem, enhanced social skills
Intensive outpatient (IOP) and day treatment	May last 1–2 months
	No use of AOD Regular program attendance
	No illegal behavior
	Obtain suitable job and lifestyle pursuits
	Obtain a suitable living situation in an AOD-free environment
Outpatient treatment	Meets every week or every other week for varying lengths of time
	Gain the ability to maintain a sober and crime-free lifestyle with minimal treatment support
	Begin attending self-help groups
Aftercare	Meets monthly
	Gain the ability to maintain sober lifestyle with no treatment support

WHERE TO GO TO FIND HELP

There are many places you can go to find help. First, you can contact your local community mental health agency. They may be able to provide AOD treatment services to you directly or give you a referral to another local agency. Second, if you are under the care of a primary care physician (PCP), you can ask that person for a referral. Generally, it is a good idea to involve your PCP in your treatment for AOD abuse whenever possible. Finally, you can find credible treatment referrals on the World Wide Web from the Substance Abuse Mental Health Services Administration at www.findtreatment.samhsa.gov.

SELF-HELP AND MUTUAL-HELP GROUPS

In addition to treatment, many people recovering from an AOD problem find it helpful to attend some sort of self-help or mutual-help group. These are groups where several people with similar problems meet to help themselves and each other to be successful in their recovery. The most widely known self-help group is Alcoholics Anonymous (AA). As stated in the AA literature:

> Alcoholics Anonymous is an international fellowship of men and women who have had a drinking problem. It is nonprofessional, self-supporting, non-denominational, multi-racial, apolitical, and available almost everywhere. There are no age or education requirements. Membership is open to anyone who wants to do something about his or her drinking problem.

AA does the following:

1. AA is open to anyone seeking help for a drinking problem. AA members share their experiences with one another in order to get and stay sober.
2. AA members provide sponsorship for one another. This is a one-on-one personal relationship between an experienced member (sponsor) and a new member. The sponsor serves as a mentor.
3. The AA model is set forth in the 12-steps.
4. The AA program helps people find ways to develop a satisfying life without alcohol.

AA offers several different meeting formats. Open meetings are open to anyone who wants to learn about AA. Closed meetings are for AA members and prospective members only. The available meeting formats are:

1. *Open speaker meetings:* open to alcoholics and nonalcoholics. Attendance at these meetings is the best way to learn about AA. At speaker meetings, an AA member tells his or her story. The speaker discusses what his or her life was like before AA, what happened, and how life changed because of AA membership.
2. *Open discussion meetings:* at these meetings one AA member speaks briefly about his or her drinking experience, and then leads a discussion on problem drinking.
3. *Closed discussion meetings:* conducted just as open discussions, but for alcoholics or prospective AA members only. All persons present at these meetings may share if they wish.
4. *Step meetings* (usually closed): discussion of one of the 12-steps.

The AA program is based on the following 12-steps. AA members "work" the steps as part of their recovery. They receive assistance from their sponsor and other AA members as they work on the steps. The 12-steps of AA are:

1. We admitted we were powerless over alcohol—that our lives had become unmanageable.
2. Came to believe that a Power greater than ourselves could restore us to sanity.

3. Made a decision to turn our will and our lives over to the care of God as we understood him.

4. Made a searching and fearless moral inventory of ourselves.

5. Admitted to God, to ourselves, and to another human being the exact nature of our wrongs.

6. Were entirely ready to have God remove all these defects of character.

7. Humbly asked God to remove our shortcomings.

8. Made a list of all persons we had harmed and became willing to make amends to them all.

9. Made direct amends to such people wherever possible, except when to do so would injure them or others.

10. Continued to take personal inventory, and when we were wrong promptly admitted it.

11. Sought through prayer and meditation to improve our conscious contact with God, as we understood Him, praying only for knowledge of His will for us and the power to carry that out.

12. Having had a spiritual awakening as the result of these steps, we tried to carry this message to alcoholics, and to practice these principles in all our affairs.

You can learn more about these steps by attending an AA meeting. The principles of AA were used to form other similar 12-step groups. These include Narcotics Anonymous (NA), Cocaine Anonymous (CA), Overeaters Anonymous (OA), Sex Addicts Anonymous (SA), Marijuana Anonymous (MA), and many more. Anyone interested in learning more about AA or other 12-step programs can access their organizational websites in the World Wide Web at:

- www.alcoholics-anonymous.org
- www.na.org
- www.ca.org
- www.oa.org
- www.marijuana-anonymous.org
- www.sa.org

In addition to AA, NA, and related 12-step–based groups, other types of support groups are also available to those working on an AOD issue. Some of these are listed below along with direct quotes from their websites stating their purposes and goals.

Moderation Management (http://www.moderation.org/)

Moderation Management (MM) is a behavioral change program and national support group network for people concerned about their drinking and who desire to make positive lifestyle changes. MM empowers individuals to accept personal responsibility for choosing and maintaining their own path, whether moderation or abstinence. MM promotes early self-recognition of risky drinking behavior, when moderate drinking is a more easily achievable goal.

Rational Recovery (http://www.rational.org/)

Rational Recovery˙ is the exclusive, worldwide source of counseling, guidance, and direct instruction on self-recovery from addiction to alcohol and other drugs through planned, permanent abstinence. We use an exclusive method, AVRT®, which is by far the most cost-effective, dignified approach of all.

Self Management and Recovery Training (http://www.smartrecovery.org/)

SMART Recovery® is a nationwide, nonprofit organization which offers free support groups to individuals who desire to gain independence from any type of addictive behavior. SMART Recovery® also offers a free Internet Message Board discussion group, and sells publications related to recovery from addictive behavior.

Secular Organizations for Sobriety (http://www.secularsobriety.org/)

Secular Organizations for Sobriety also known as Save Our Selves is dedicated to providing a path to sobriety, an alternative to those paths depending upon supernatural or religious beliefs. We respect diversity, welcome healthy skepticism, and encourage rational thinking as well as the expression of feelings.

Women for Sobriety (www.womenforsobriety.org/)

Women for Sobriety is both an organization and a self-help program for women alcoholics. It is, in fact, the first national self-help program for women alcoholics. Based upon a Thirteen Statement Program of positivity that encourages emotional and spiritual growth, the "New Life" Program has been extremely effective in helping women to overcome their alcoholism and learn a wholly new lifestyle. As a Program, it can stand alone or be used along with other programs simultaneously. It is being used not only by women alcoholics in small self-help groups but also in hospitals, clinics, treatment facilities, women centers, and wherever alcoholics are being treated.

THE NEXT STEP

Use the resources in this chapter if you think you want to explore the possibility of entering treatment. As mentioned, several options are available to you and you should take the time to choose the option that is right for you. Before you seek help, however, it may be beneficial to have a good understanding about what you want to gain from counseling. Miller and Brown developed a questionnaire titled "What I Want From Treatment" to assist potential treatment seekers with this task (this worksheet is available in the Miller, 2002 reference at the end of this book). Their questionnaire is given in Worksheet 3 at the end of this chapter. I encourage you to complete the questionnaire if you think you want to seek some help and take your responses with you when you attend your first assessment or treatment session.

CONCLUSION

You have now reached the end of this book and I applaud you for all your hard work! You reviewed a lot of important information in this book and will need to use these skills as you continue to make change happen in your life. As you maintain the changes you have made, go back and review the chapters in this book from time to time. It's human nature to forget important things we have learned, and reviewing the material in this book several times will help ensure that the material "sticks" and keep you firmly in the maintenance stage of change. Finally, remember that you should not give up if you do not experience immediate success in your recovery efforts. As I mentioned earlier, this book and other forms of self-help and treatment are not effective for everyone. Keep searching for the best form of help for you. When you find something that works, do more of it. Most important of all, however, be sure to celebrate the changes you make and recognize the progress you have created! Good luck in achieving your goals, and I wish you success.

Worksheet 1: The Maintenance Stage

Fill in the spaces below to identify examples of how you are keeping the changes you have made permanent. If you do not feel you are currently in the maintenance stage of change, write down examples of how you think you would act if you were in the maintenance stage.

I demonstrate a commitment to a new, alcohol and drug-free life by:

_____

_____

_____

_____

_____

_____

_____

I show a strong determination to stick to my change plan by:

_____

_____

_____

_____

_____

_____

_____

_____

I consistently take part in the following new and interesting activities:

_____

_____

_____

_____

_____

_____

_____

_____

Worksheet 2: My Life in Five Years

Answer the questions below to identify what your future looks like after you have met your goals relative to your alcohol and drug use.

Chapter 1

I identified the following as my goals for change:

_____

_____

_____

_____

Now that it is 5 years later, my life looks like:

_____

_____

_____

_____

Chapter 2

I identified the following specific behaviors that I wanted to change:

_____

_____

_____

_____

Now that it is 5 years later, my life looks like:

_____

_____

_____

_____

Chapters 3 and 4

I identified the following dysfunctional thinking patterns and thinking errors that I have made:

_____

_____

_____

_____

Now that it is 5 years later, my thinking looks like:

_____

_____

_____

_____

Chapter 5

I created the following goals for my holistic recovery lifestyle:

_____

_____

_____

_____

Now that it is 5 years later, my life looks like:

_____

_____

_____

_____

Chapter 6

My relapse prevention plan included ideas for handling the following high-risk situations:

_____

_____

_____

_____

Now that it is 5 years later, I manage these high-risk situations by:

_____

_____

_____

_____

Chapter 7

The emotions I identified as having the most trouble with were:

_____

_____

_____

_____

Now that it is 5 years later, I manage these high-risk situations by:

_____

_____

_____

_____

Chapter 8

A life of integrity looks like:

_____

_____

_____

_____

_____

_____

_____

_____

_____

_____

_____

_____

Now that it is 5 years later, I live a life of integrity by:

_____

_____

_____

_____

Summary

Overall all I would describe my new life as:

_____

_____

_____

_____

_____

_____

_____

_____

_____

_____

_____

_____

_____

_____

_____

Worksheet 3. What I Want From Treatment (2.0)

Instructions

People have different ideas about what they want, need, and expect from treatment. This questionnaire is designed to help you explain what you would like to have happen in your treatment.

Now that it is 5 years later, my experience of these emotions is:

Many possibilities are listed. For each one, please indicate how much you would like for this to be part of your treatment. You can do this by circling one number (0, 1, 2, or 3) for each item. This is what the numbers mean:

0	NO	*This means that you definitely do NOT want or need this from treatment.*
1	?	*This means that you are UNSURE. MAYBE you want or need this from treatment.*
2	Yes	*This means that you DO want or need this from treatment.*
3	YES!	*This means that you DEFINITELY want or need this from treatment.*

For Example:

Consider item #1 which says, "I want to receive detoxification."

If you definitely do NOT want or need to receive detoxification, you would circle 0.

If you are UNSURE whether you want or need detoxification, you would circle 1.

If you DO want detoxification, you would circle 2.

If you DEFINITELY know that detoxification is an important goal for your treatment, you would circle 3.

If you have any questions about how to use this questionnaire, ask for assistance before you begin.

Section I: Addictive behaviors

Do you want this from treatment?	NO 0	Maybe 1	Yes 2	YES! 3
1. I want to receive detoxification, to ease my withdrawal from alcohol or other drugs.	0	1	2	3
2. I want to find out for sure whether I have a problem with alcohol or other drugs.	0	1	2	3
3. I want help to stop drinking alcohol completely.	0	1	2	3
4. I want help to decrease my drinking.	0	1	2	3
5. I want help to stop using drugs (other than alcohol).	0	1	2	3
6. I want help to decrease my use of drugs (other than alcohol).	0	1	2	3
7. I want to stop using tobacco.	0	1	2	3
8. I want to decrease my use of tobacco.	0	1	2	3
9. I want help with an eating problem.	0	1	2	3
10. I want help with a gambling problem.	0	1	2	3
11. I want to take Antabuse (a medication to help me stop drinking).	0	1	2	3
12. I want to take Trexan (a medication to help me stop using heroin).	0	1	2	3
13. I want to take methadone.	0	1	2	3
14. I want to learn more about alcohol/drug problems.	0	1	2	3
15. I want to learn some skills to keep from returning to alcohol or other drugs.	0	1	2	3
16. I would like to learn more about 12-step programs like Alcoholics Anonymous (AA) or Narcotics Anonymous (NA).	0	1	2	3

Worksheet 3. What I Want From Treatment (2.0) (continued)

Section II: Other concerns

Do you want this from treatment?	NO 0	Maybe 1	Yes 2	YES! 3
17. I would like to talk about some personal problems.	0	1	2	3
18. I need to fulfill a requirement of the courts.	0	1	2	3
19. I would like help with problems in my marriage or close relationship.	0	1	2	3
20. I want help with some health problems.	0	1	2	3
21. I want help to decrease my stress and tension.	0	1	2	3
22. I would like to improve my health by learning more about nutrition and exercise.	0	1	2	3
23. I want help with depression or moodiness.	0	1	2	3
24. I want to work on my spiritual growth.	0	1	2	3
25. I want to learn how to solve problems in my life.	0	1	2	3
26. I want help with angry feelings and how I express them.	0	1	2	3
27. I want to have healthier relationships.	0	1	2	3
28. I would like to discuss sexual problems.	0	1	2	3
29. I want to learn how to express my feelings in a more healthy way.	0	1	2	3
30. I want to learn how to relax better.	0	1	2	3
31. I want help in overcoming boredom.	0	1	2	3
32. I want help with feelings of loneliness.	0	1	2	3
33. I want to discuss having been physically abused.	0	1	2	3
34. I want help to prevent violence at home.	0	1	2	3
35. I want to discuss having been sexually abused.	0	1	2	3
36. I want to work on having better self-esteem.	0	1	2	3
37. I want help with sleep problems.	0	1	2	3
38. I want help with legal problems.	0	1	2	3

Worksheet 3. What I Want From Treatment (2.0) (continued)

Do you want this from treatment?	NO 0	Maybe 1	Yes 2	YES! 3
39. I want advice about financial problems.	0	1	2	3
40. I would like help in finding a place to live.	0	1	2	3
41. I could use help in finding a job.	0	1	2	3
42. I want help in overcoming shyness.	0	1	2	3
43. Someone close to me has died or left, and I would like to talk about it.	0	1	2	3
44. I have thoughts about suicide and would like to discuss this.	0	1	2	3
45. I want help with personal fears or anxieties.	0	1	2	3
46. I want help to be a better parent.	0	1	2	3
47. I feel very confused and would like help with this.	0	1	2	3
48. I would like information about or testing for HIV/AIDS.	0	1	2	3
49. I want someone to listen to me.	0	1	2	3
50. I want to learn to have fun without drugs or alcohol.	0	1	2	3
51. I want someone to tell me what to do.	0	1	2	3
52. I want help in setting goals and priorities in my life.	0	1	2	3
53. I would like to learn how to manage my time better.	0	1	2	3
54. I want help to receive SSI/disability payments.	0	1	2	3
55. I want to find enjoyable ways to spend my free time.	0	1	2	3
56. I want help in getting my child(ren) back.	0	1	2	3
57. I would like to talk about my past.	0	1	2	3
58. I need help in getting motivated to change.	0	1	2	3

Worksheet 3. What I Want From Treatment (2.0) (continued)

Section III: About the kind of treatment

Do you want this from treatment?	NO 0	Maybe 1	Yes 2	YES! 3
59. I would like to see a female counselor.	0	1	2	3
60. I would like to see a male counselor.	0	1	2	3
61. I would like to see the counselor I had before.	0	1	2	3
62. I would like to see a doctor or nurse about medical problems.	0	1	2	3
63. I want to receive medication.	0	1	2	3
64. I would like my spouse or partner to be in treatment with me.	0	1	2	3
65. I would like to have private, individual counseling.	0	1	2	3
66. I would like to be in a group with people who are dealing with problems similar to my own.	0	1	2	3
67. I need someone to care for my children while I am in treatment.	0	1	2	3
68. I want my treatment to be short.	0	1	2	3
69. I believe I will need to be in treatment for a long time.	0	1	2	3

Is there anything else that you would like from treatment? If so, please write it here:

_____

_____

_____

_____

_____

Source: This instrument was obtained from: Miller, W. (2002). Enhancing motivation to change in substance abuse treatment. Treatment improvement protocol series, Tip 35. Rockville, MD: U.S. Department of Health and Human Services and is in the public domain.

REFERENCES

Beck, A., Wright, F., Newman, C., & Liese, B. (2001). *Cognitive therapy of substance abuse.* New York: Guilford.

Berg, I. K., & Miller, S. D. (1992). *Working with the problem drinker: A solution-focused approach.* New York: W. W. Norton.

Berg, I. K. & Miller, S. D. (1995). *The miracle method: A radically new approach to problem drinking.* New York: Norton.

Connors, G., Donovan, D., & DiClemente, C. (2000). *Substance abuse treatment and the stages of change.* New York: Guilford.

Doweiko, H. (2005). *Concepts of chemical dependency* (5th ed.). Pacific Grove, CA: Wadsworth.

Ellis, A (2001). *Overcoming destructive beliefs, feelings, and behaviors: New directions for Rational Emotive Behavior Therapy.* New York: Prometheus Books.

Evans, K., & Sullivan, J. (2001). *Dual diagnosis: Counseling the mentally ill substance abuser* (2nd ed.). New York: Guilford.

Epstein, J., Barker, P., Vorburger, M., & Murtha, C. (2002). *Serious mental illness and its co-occurrence with substance use disorders, 2002.* Washington, DC: Department of Health and Human Services, Substance Abuse and Mental Health Services Administration, Office of Applied Studies.

Hazelden. (2002). *Socialization: A cognitive behavioral treatment curriculum.* Center City, MN: Hazelden Press.

Johnson, D. (2003). *Reaching out: Interpersonal effectiveness and self-actualization* (8th ed.). New York: Allyn and Bacon.

Kolb, D. (1981). Learning style and disciplinary differences. In A. W. Chickering and Associates, *The modern American college* (pp. 232–255). San Francisco: Jossey-Bass.

Marlatt, G. (2002). *Harm reduction: Pragmatic strategies for managing high-risk behaviors.* New York: Guilford.

Marlatt, G., & Donovan, D. (2005). *Relapse prevention: maintenance strategies in the treatment of addictive behaviors* (2nd ed.). New York: Guilford.

Michigan Department of Corrections. (2001). *Advanced Substance Abuse Treatment: Cognitive Skills for Addicted Offenders.* Lansing, MI: Author.

Miller, W. (2002). *Enhancing motivation to change in substance abuse treatment.* Treatment improvement protocol series, Tip 35. Rockville, MD: U.S. Department of Health and Human Services.

Miller, W., & Munoz, R. (2005). *Controlling your drinking: Tools to make moderation work for you.* New York: Guilford.

Miller, W. & Rollnick, S. (2001). *Motivational interviewing: Preparing people for change* (2nd ed.). New York: Guilford.

National Institute on Drug Abuse. A cognitive-behavioral approach: Treating cocaine addiction. Available at: www.nida.nih.gov.

Prochaska, J. & DiClemente, C. (1994). *The transtheoretical approach: Crossing traditional boundaries of therapy.* Melbourne, FL: Krieger.

Reilly, P. & Shopshire, M. (2002). *Anger management for substance abuse and mental health clients: A cognitive behavioral therapy manual.* Rockville, MD: U.S. Department of Health and Human Services, SAMHSA, CSAT.

Samenow, S. (2004). *Inside the criminal mind.* New York: Random House.

U.S. Department of Health and Human Services. (2002). *Relapse prevention and the substance abusing criminal offender: Treatment assistance publication 8.* Washington DC: SAMHSA.

U.S. Department of Health and Human Services. (2004). *Counselor's manual for relapse prevention with chemically dependent criminal offenders, Treatment assistance publication 19.* Washington, DC: SAMHSA.

Velasquez, M., Maurer, G., Crouch, C., & DiClemente, C. (2001). *Group treatment for substance abuse: A stages-of-change therapy manual.* New York: Guilford.

Wanberg, K. & Milkman, H. (1998). *Criminal conduct and substance abuse treatment.* New York: Sage.

Wegscheider-Cruse, S. (1989). *Another chance: Hope and health for the alcoholic family.* Palo Alto, CA: Science and Behavior Books.

INDEX